WIN the RELATIONSHIP, not the DEAL

Six Common Sense Strategies To Succeed In Life & Business

Casey Jacox

Copyright ©2020 by Casey Jacox

All Rights Reserved.

Published in the United States by

7 Stones Publishing, Queen Creek, Arizona

Library of Congress Cataloguing-in-Publication Data

LCCN: 2019955165

ISBN: 978-0-9993714-9-7 (Paperback)

Printed in the United States of America

www.7stonespublishing.com

10 9 8 7 6 5 4 3 2 1

First Edition

This book is dedicated to my beautiful wife, Carrie. You are the rock of our family and none of my business success would have ever happened without your support at home. To my children, Ryder and Rylee. You might not understand truly what dad did for his job, but I worked hard to provide you a life I never knew was possible.

TABLE OF CONTENTS

Foreword - Written by Dr. James Gaudino, President of Central Washington University – *vii*

Introduction – *1*

Chapter 1 - Follow the Golden Rule. Always. - *11*

Chapter 2 – Always Set Proper Expectations. - *35*

Chapter 3 – Don't Just Hear Your Customers, Listen To Them. - *51*

Chapter 4 – Always Document And Follow Up. - *69*

Chapter 5 – Ditch The Ego And Let Your Authentic Self Shine! - *95*

Chapter 6 – Success Takes Time – Be Patient And Persistent! - *137*

Chapter 7 – Win The Relationship – Personal Life Examples Beyond Selling. - *153*

Chapter 8 – Finish Strong! Putting It All Together: Winning Your Relationships. - *167*

FOREWORD

Casey Jacox and I agree that relationships are essential elements of success in business and in life. His understanding of relationship building is why I asked him to be a director on the Central Washington University Foundation Board. The function of that organization is similar to selling, with a critical difference: the monetary transaction is unilateral. Donors voluntarily give of their wealth with no expectation of material return. The model is solely reliant on relationships and trust.

Our understanding of the critical role of relationships and trust have similar origins. Like him, I played football in my younger years. He was the star quarterback; I was the unsung offensive lineman. While we played on different teams more and more than a decade apart (I'm the older), those experiences demonstrated to us that the only path to success was to work together. I had to know where he was going to be, and he had to understand that I would do everything I could to keep the defense away from that spot on the field. That level of teamwork mandated understanding of the needs and plans each had and trust that each would to their part. That relationship, often labeled "chemistry" in sports, is what Casey writes about.

I encourage all to take a moment to read the dedication Casey offers to his business team and to his family. His offering of credit, gratitude, and hope are clearly indications of the authenticity of the author and the sincerity of the person I have come to know.

It would have been my pleasure to block for him during our playing days. It is now an honor for me to know him and to work with him.

James L. Gaudino, PhD
President, Central Washington University

CHAPTER 1:

Follow The Golden Rule. Always.

When my son was seven years old, he asked me, *"Daddy, what do you do for your job?"* I was perplexed. I couldn't tell him that I provided recruiting, staff augmentation, or professional services, since those things meant nothing to him. Instead, I told him that I made friends for a living. Yes, that's correct. I told him I made friends for a living.

You might laugh like my buddies did when I told them. However, when you stop and think about my response, you realize that is what elite salespeople do – they make friends with their customers. They treat their customers like family members or best friends. They always make their customers feel like the most important person in the room. They always follow through with genuine intent to help solve their customers' problems.

In other words, great sellers follow the Golden Rule, treating others as they would want to be treated. It's one of the oldest and most impactful pieces of advice.

When I reflect on the Golden Rule, I think *genuine*, *vulnerable*, *unselfish*, *compassionate*, *empathetic,* and *patient.* Treating others as you would want them to treat you will never go out of style. Any ingenuine behavior, will unfortunately shine through to your customer or colleague. You must be vulnerable enough to let others see who you are as a person. When you think of other people's feelings before your own, you're being unselfish.

To treat others the way you want to be treated requires compassion and the ability to empathize. Your customer or teammate might do things that upset you, but you must always try to give them the benefit of the doubt. Meaning, one must understand that when someone acts in a negative light, their intent might not be to be destructive or purposely deceitful. Instead of responding in anger, try answering with a question to understand the intent of their message.

For example, your customer might question your sincerity. He might say, "Is she only interested in closing the deal?" Or she might say, "Why is he pushing me so hard to make a decision?"

This might all sound like common sense, but it is not commonly practiced.

The Golden Rule continues to be taught not only because of its value, but also because people struggle to implement it. When we forget this timeless rule, our relationships become turbulent and fall apart.

Examples of the value of leading with empathy have been around us for centuries. One of my all-time favorite leaders, Abraham Lincoln, reminds me that doing the right thing is timeless.

Abraham Lincoln provides many extraordinary examples of humility in leadership. Famously, Lincoln didn't just want to end slavery, he wanted to save the Union, too. He applied the Golden Rule when dealing with the South in an effort to understand Southerners and to keep the Union whole. Of the people who made personal appeals to him while he was president, Lincoln once said, "They do not want much, and they get very little. Each one considers his business of great importance, and I must gratify them. I know how I would feel in their place[1]."

During Lincoln's presidency, women and minorities were not treated equally, and yet Lincoln's use of empathy allowed him to find ways to put himself in others' shoes. He treated others the way he wanted to be treated, which helped him build many relationships. For example, he encouraged a woman who would have been unrightfully convicted of murder to flee. Finally, he was willing to listen, both to mothers pleading for their sons, and to people sentenced to death.

A more lighthearted but still impactful story unfolds in the 1984 movie, *The Karate Kid*. In the film, Daniel (played by Ralph Macchio) had moved from New Jersey to California. As the new kid, Daniel finds himself being picked on by kids from the Cobra Kai Karate School. Mr. Miyagi, a frail-looking older man, breaks up one of his most unfortunate beatings using karate. Daniel decides he wants to learn karate so that he can seek revenge against the bullies from Cobra Kai. Instead, Mr. Miyagi teaches Daniel that if you learn karate to seek revenge, you dig two graves: your enemy's and your own. Whenever Daniel attempts to hurt others or not treat others well, he ends up hurting himself. When he practices compassion and patience, situations can change for the better. Just like in business, we always have to remember to treat others the way we want to be treated if we want successful outcomes.

We don't always see this lesson in the short run, but we feel it in the long run. This is another reason I've found that winning the relationship is always better than winning a deal. Once I changed my mindset to be more customer centric, I won more

INTRODUCTION

Today's fast-paced digital world is overflowing with experts armed with a variety of tools to help you become the best salesperson possible. These so-called experts provide advice making you believe by implementing minor changes, you will be able to increase sales dramatically overnight. Unfortunately, there isn't a magic phrase or potion that a salesperson can use to reach instant success. It takes time. You must be ready and committed to do the little things each and every day.

Imagine a day in the future when the ability to build relationships becomes more natural—almost effortless and easier for you. On that day, you will know the best behavior for creating more sustainable relationships and positive outcomes, not only in your professional life, but also in your personal life.

That day will only come if you're committed to becoming a lifelong learner. Someone who is always seeking ways to improve your skillset. A person who can take feedback — both positive and negative. A devoted individual who can stay focused on building meaningful relationships with your colleagues and your customers. You should never be satisfied with the status quo and must always strive to be your best. Successful salespeople are humble; they never stop looking for ways to grow, even after a great month or a huge year of impactful sales results.

They aren't afraid to speak up when something isn't right. When they do, their approach is always communicated in a way that respects their listeners. They use the proper tone for a given situation and stay in command of their message when communicating with anyone they come in contact with. While some of these traits might be inborn, you *can* learn them. This book will teach you how.

If you've become frustrated in your sales career and wish you could gain real-world advice from someone who has built hundreds of successful relationships, this book is for you. If you've been too intimidated to approach the office and face your own selling flaws, or too afraid to pick up the phone, this book is for you. If you've had to rebuild your book of business once, twice, maybe multiple times, this book is for you. If you've found some success in your sales career, but you are still fighting the daily ebbs and flows of a sales career, this book certainly is for you. If you've managed a sales team and found yourself more concerned with the number of dials your sellers made versus the number of customers won, this book is for you. I've personally seen and faced these sales challenges head on throughout my career and found ways to persevere.

I wrote this book to help salespeople succeed in business and in life. This book is less about getting more sales and more about winning valuable lifelong relationships that will then lead to more sales. I want to help you achieve the best kind of successes—ones that help you reach your goals and make you feel good about yourself and the relationships you're building. This philosophy of "winning people" has helped me achieve fantastic success in my business life, and I want to teach it to others.

Most importantly, I am writing this book for my 23-year-old self. When I entered the business world, I was young and acted the way too many salespeople do. I focused solely on the transactional way of doing business. Sure, I knew the job was about people and building relationships, but I didn't have the core foundational relationship and sales skills needed for long term success. The good news for you as my reader is that I will teach you fundamental sales skills to help you succeed in your career.

Too often, I was focused on the metrics of sales activities rather than understanding what makes a great salesperson. I would focus on how many phone calls I had made that day, or how many emails I had sent. Don't get me wrong; those are essential tasks in the everyday life of a seller. However, they are not the most important. This book will teach you the most important task: creating quality interactions with potential customers. You will learn to work smarter and focus on what really matters in life – building authentic relationships that will last.

I eventually learned about the power of consultative and relationship selling through the ups and downs of my industry and my business. Earlier in my selling career, I thought success would never happen, and then—BOOM!—the flood gates opened and customers from everywhere were buying. All of my hard work started to pay off, and it was a great feeling. But then I became complacent, as we often do when we've had a little success. My business started to slow down.

I wasn't focused on growing new relationships and I was left with long-standing customers that were reducing their spend rather than increasing it. This up-and-down cycle is common in many industries. I found that if I always pushed myself to keep my sales pipeline full of opportunities, then my success was more consistent and sustainable.

To retain customers, you have to build a relationship with them—show them you understand their business needs and will work to meet or exceed their expectations, even if you won't benefit as much.

You are slowly showing your customer they are more important than the sale.

Focusing on transactions means you're not on your customer's shortlist – one of the top two or three vendors they would call first. They see you not as someone who is there to help them grow their business, but as someone willing to sacrifice the customer in favor of making the sale. Unfortunately, this behavior is common for the average salesperson. This short-term view is called transactional selling. It's when sellers go to any length to win a deal, even if they lose the relationship with their customer. They're concerned with that one transaction and not potential future transactions. Transactional sellers are reluctant to acknowledge the long-term frustration they are causing themselves in favor of short-term success. They might be working hard, but they are not working smart. Too often, sellers could prevent future struggles by focusing on relationships first and business transactions second.

Sales leaders sometimes help create this problem. They micromanage their teams, standing over their sales reps to ensure they make a set number of calls per day. Regardless of the outcome, all the sales leader cares about is how many calls or connections you make. *For whose benefit and why?*

This sales method is flawed. Companies that follow it shouldn't be surprised when their sales professionals earn a terrible reputation, nor should they be surprised with consistent turnover inside their sales organization. These sales leaders create so much pressure to sell and grow a sales territory that their sales reps are willing to annoy prospects with constant calls, use high-pressure sales tactics, and sell something that isn't right for the customer. And they'll do it at a pace that quickly leads to burnout and high turnover rates.

Leaders who model and teach core skills for building authentic relationships while still encouraging output, will see positive results. Selling should be about creating sustainable revenue by growing respectful, active business relationships. I've always loved sales managers who pushed for high call volumes, but with the emphasis on the quality of each call, not the quantity. When salespeople and business leaders fail to think about selling in that light, customers become frustrated and look for other places to invest their dollars. I was living proof of this earlier in my career. Once I learned the value of building relationships, I vowed to teach others these positive results.

In this book, you'll learn to focus on winning more relationships, which will help increase your number of deals. You will gain crucial relationship-building skills that will reduce turnover and increase employee satisfaction. If reading that excites you, you are ready to invest in yourself. You are ready to learn how to close your gaps so that you can become the salesperson or sales leader everyone wants to emulate.

Imagine this day in the future: You're in a meeting, and in front of your entire team, your manager uses you as the example of how to grow your business successfully year-in and year-out. Your manager praises you for your ability to always be prepared and to do the little things correctly. He or she highlights the glowing customer reviews you received during your latest quarterly business review.

How does this make you feel? Can you imagine the confidence you'll have? Keep reading, and I will get you to that day.

This journey won't be comfortable, nor will it be a get-rich-quick plan. Instead, you'll start on a career-long journey through real-life examples and lessons that will help you create a relationship-focused culture that will sustain you through any turbulent waters. You'll learn the strategies and skills needed to win relationships. You'll learn how to keep yourself on the path and focus on your goals without harming others along the way.

You might be saying, "Casey, this is great, but I don't have time. My boss needs me to close five deals each day." I get it.

The pressure to close deals mounts every day. But as someone once told me, "You have to slow down sometimes to go fast in business." I'm proof that you can sell at an elite level and exceed your financial goals by selling the right way. The right way is always about the customer, not about the seller.

At the end of this book, you will help shape a new culture in your sales team as others will start to adopt your selling approach. You will learn to stay true to your authentic self rather than being the smile-and-dial salesperson who is in the business for the wrong reasons. I'm excited to share my successes with you. More importantly, I'm excited to share my failures because they will demonstrate so clearly what not to do and why winning the relationship is more important. I'm not perfect; I still make many mistakes. But it's part of the process.

You'll learn all of this through common sense strategies that have helped me become Kforce's all-time leading salesperson in the 57-year history of the company. It doesn't matter what you were born with or the circumstances you found yourself in. If you have a growth mindset (or are willing to commit to building a growth mindset), you will overcome your challenges.

You can reach goals you only dreamed of achieving. For example, I wasn't the smartest kid growing up, nor was I the fastest or the toughest on the athletic field. I didn't go to an Ivy League school. In fact, I joke about going to the Harvard of the West Coast—Central Washington University (CWU). I didn't study writing in college. I became a writer through personal and professional experience, both through successes and failures. But my moments of failure and hardship propelled me to success, and yours will do the same for you once you know how to leverage them.

The mindset I'm always striving for—the one I want to teach you—is growth. We can use our moments of failure and hardship to propel us into future success. As my college football coach John Zamberlin said,

"Every day you have a choice to get better. No one ever stays the same; you are either getting better or getting worse."

You'll read about my heroes and influences throughout the book. (The Resources section at the back compiles them for you.) The lessons you will learn are not things I created, but are guiding strategies that propelled me to great success. We can all be on a path to growth each day, if we choose.

True mastery will never be achieved in life, but if we have the humility to own our mistakes and work hard to fix those gaps, we will dramatically increase the relationships in our lives. After you finish reading this book, you will understand how to......

WIN the RELATIONSHIP, not the DEAL.

relationships and generated more deals over the long term.

Sales guru and author, Brian Tracy, wrote a brief but impactful article highlighting the importance of the Golden Rule in authentic relationship building. In his article, Tracy describes the importance of caring about your customers. Top sales professionals, he says, "carry themselves as advisors, mentors and friends. They become emotionally involved in their transactions[2]." More importantly, he says, they dedicate themselves to providing ideal solutions to their customer's *actual* needs. Tracy's mindset and philosophy have taught many to focus on the customer's needs.

Put this book down for a minute and ask yourself: When was the last time someone went out of the way to be kind to you? How about the last time someone listened intently to what you had to say? Or would talk less about themselves and be more interested in you? When was the last time *you* went out of your way to be kind to someone without expecting anything in return? How good of a listener were you? Hopefully, you were able to think of examples where you did a great job or found areas to improve as it relates to leading by the Golden Rule.

On the flip side, when was the last time someone was a complete jerk to you? Or someone didn't listen to you because they were so distracted with something else? As we all know, those experiences don't leave a good taste in your mouth. You feel less important and will see relationships erode.

Whether you want to follow the Golden Rule is a personal choice. If you're genuinely committed to advancing your selling career, decide *today* to always follow the Golden Rule. The elite sellers I've worked and studied with also possessed great leadership experience by living the Golden Rule day in and day out. Not just with their customers, but with everyone they came in contact with. The Golden Rule creates positive environments and attracts positive energetic outcomes.

Why Is This Important To You As A Seller?

During my sales career, I've found that productive, successful sellers follow the Golden Rule. They are curious in nature, optimistic, intelligent, and level-headed, all of which helps them treat others the way they want to be treated. It allows them to do what Orison Swett Marden, successful entrepreneur and inspirational author, advised in the late 19th century. Not only did Marden hold many academic degrees, but he also could see a societal need that he could solve from a business perspective.

In 1897, he created *Success Magazine,* which focused on self-culture, personal development, and principles of success. It would eventually grow to a subscription base of nearly half a million subscribers. It was a pretty amazing achievement for the time. Just imagine how successful Marden would've been if he had access to the TED stage.

One thing about Marden that stood out to me was his ability to see the power of connecting authentically with the customer, as well as the power of patience and perseverance. Nearly 100 years have passed, and some businesses still don't understand the positive outcomes you can generate by treating others the way you want to be treated.

> **"The Golden Rule for every businessman is this: Put yourself in your customer's place."**
> -Orison Swett Marden-

Marden's childhood was marked by tragedy. His mother died when he was three, and his father died when he was seven. He then lived with one guardian after another, often working as their "hired boy." The traumatic stress he must have experienced is awful to imagine, yet somehow Marden used these difficulties to create a positive mindset.

As we saw in the *Karate Kid* example, had Marden given in to feeling sorry for himself or getting wrapped up in negative feelings would only have kept him from progressing. Instead, he put his energies into changing his life, earning several academic degrees.

What is truly amazing is that Marden didn't write his first book until he was 44 years old. His first book, *Pushing to the Front*, was lost in a hotel fire before being published. Although heartbroken, he persevered. Instead of thinking the world was against him, he went down the street and purchased an inexpensive notebook and began re-writing his manuscript. *Pushing to the Front* was eventually published in 1894, and Marden succeeded in his life goal of writing his dream book.

Pushing to the Front was the most successful personal development book of its time, receiving praise from American presidents William McKinley and Theodore Roosevelt. A man who lost his parents and almost died in a hotel fire showed the world the power of not letting one's adverse circumstances impact one's way of life, attitude, or treatment of others.

Despite all of Marden's adversity and obstacles, he stayed true to his core principles. He was selfless and thought of others often. He wrote, "We make the world we live in and shape our own environment."

In today's fast-paced world, which requires us to always be connected to technology, we rarely take time to breathe and think through what comes out of our mouth. We also don't take into account what our body language is saying. As salespeople, we work in environments where egos can grow quite large and impact the culture. But, we can shape our environment as Marden did if we are self-aware and choose words that will show others respect. In doing so, we will significantly increase our chances of winning more relationships, both internally and externally.

One of my favorite books of all time regarding the Golden Rule is Stephen Covey's *Seven Habits of Highly Effective People*. It provides great wisdom for business professionals and excellent advice on the art of building relationships. One of Covey's fundamental rules is to always begin with the end in mind. By thinking long term, you will focus on creating a positive outcome when having human interactions. Before you respond to a customer, ask yourself what you want out of the situation. For many, including myself, being self-aware enough to control our emotions is a challenge. But by thinking long term, you will help prevent a negative impact on your relationships.

Let me give you an example. In the first year of my selling career, I worked for BarCodes West (now ID Label), a label manufacturer —although my naivety allowed me to call them stickers. As a competitor, I was relentless on the phone and would dial and dial and dial, not sure of what I was going to say. My competitive spirit always took me to the limits that first year. My outbound-call list of sales prospects was always extraordinarily long. I found that customers rarely picked up the phone, which tested my patience. It took a lot of positive mindset training to ensure I stayed positive and focused. As I went through this struggle, so many of my life experiences helped me stay the course. Specifically, I reflected back to my days of training for football conditioning tests and to push through the pain or struggle to ensure I would achieve my goal. However, I was not perfect and would learn some valuable lessons. There were times that I let my frustrations get to me, and I would get short with my teammates. I wouldn't always give them the benefit of the doubt for mistakes or misunderstandings. This damaged the trust within the team, and I had to learn to grow up to be the teammate I was striving to be. This was just another reminder of why I needed to follow the Golden Rule.

Letting those frustrations get to me also damaged customer relationships. At the end of the day, after making 70 or more fruitless calls, I would be surprised when a customer finally did pick up. It's never good for a customer to hear surprise in your voice; they want to buy from salespeople who instill confidence in what they are selling or solving for the customer.

I should've been making sure I was fully prepared for each phone call, always expecting the potential clients to pick up the phone.

I had to train myself to always keep confidence in my voice by recording some of my sales calls. Some of you might cringe when you read that, but it worked! My leader helped me understand that to truly get better, you have to be willing to look for your gaps—and not only see them, but also truly hear them. This sales training reminded me of my days of playing college football where we would always watch film from a practice or game to see what we did well and where we could improve.

One of the best ways to keep the confidence in my voice was to maintain a positive attitude and mindset. Those days of intense cold-calling encouraged me to build a foundation as a successful salesperson. As hard as it was, I appreciated the lessons I learned that first year of selling and embraced the memories that were made.

Each day, we have many interactions with co-workers and clients. And yet, in my 43 years on this earth, I haven't met anyone who said, "I can't wait to wake up tomorrow and ruin someone's day." People make mistakes, they have motivations we can't see, and they experience a full range of emotions, just as you and I do daily. Instead of responding in anger, give your teammate or customer the benefit of the doubt first. By consistently trying to give colleagues the benefit of the doubt, you will help shape a culture of forgiveness in your company. Leading by example when times get fierce or intense allows you as a leader and salesperson to set the tone for your internal environment. When your boss is pressuring you to make your sales numbers, your bank account is low, and your co-worker is aggressively pursuing your client, it can be difficult to see a way to create a positive outcome. But, if you don't think about the Golden Rule, especially in times of conflict, sooner or later, your actions will only create a negative environment.

Luckily, I had the chance to hear a gentleman named Mike Robbins speak. One of his most powerful statements hit home: "Be yourself, everyone else is already taken."

If you struggle to be your genuine self in finding ways to create a positive outcome, especially in times of conflict, sooner or later someone will question your motives—and that "someone" is often your customer. They will dump you in the category of "typical salesperson" and limit their interactions with you, stunting the potential relationship with them.

While this principle isn't the easiest to follow, it will be one of the most impactful to your personal and professional life. Following it takes honest self-awareness and the ability to realize when your emotions might be getting the best of you, which is easier said than done. Asking for coaching, maybe from a teammate or manager, can help you become self-aware, and then you will begin to find new success in your ability to build and maintain relationships.

Try This Exercise

Early in my career, I learned to write things down if I wanted to make them happen. Periodically, I'm going to ask you to do a short writing exercise—no more than 5–10 minutes, I promise! By doing these small exercises, you'll internalize the lessons and see the connections to your work and life. I hope you try them.

Write down the last time you lost your cool and said something negative or insulting to a teammate. How would you describe the interaction? How did it make you feel? Did you admit your mistake to your teammate, or did you pretend that it wasn't that big of a deal and move on? Read over what you wrote. How does seeing the words in print make you feel now? Does it make you wonder what you could've done differently? If you don't feel good about how you treated your teammate, your subconscious may be nudging you toward the Golden Rule in business and in life.

When our goal is to build long-term relationships, it is essential to ask ourselves two questions:

- How did my actions make the other person feel?

- Did my actions help build trust with the other person, or did my actions take our relationship back a step?

When we fail to control how we communicate with someone, we must reflect on the situation. The writing exercise you just finished can help you analyze your actions. It's similar to my college football experience of reviewing game or practice footage. That was when we truly learned because we couldn't hide from our mistakes: the film always told the truth. If we apply this same philosophy of "watching film" to ourselves, the impact we could have on our interactions would be enormous. Analyzing our actions every day may not be practical, but whenever we do reflect on how we say and do things, we can shape our environment in a positive way, just like Marden, and build and strengthen our relationships.

An essential part of living the Golden Rule in winning relationships has to do with trust. Customers want to do business with people they trust. It's hard to build trust if you don't always treat people with the respect and understanding you would expect from someone who is selling to you. Guy Kawasaki, venture capitalist, technologist, and former Apple executive, once said:

> *"Enchantment is the purest form of sales. Enchantment is all about changing people's hearts, minds, and actions because you provide them a vision or a way to do things better. The difference between enchantment and simple sales is that with enchantment, you have the other person's best interests at heart, too."*

When you always think about your customers or colleagues first, you will dramatically increase your chance of winning more relationships.

How can you accomplish this task? Let me show you. Almost every time I call a customer, I review the notes of our previous interactions so I can ask questions about them personally or about their business. These questions show them that I am listening and truly care about them.

One of my customers was a huge fan of the North Dakota State Football (NDSU) program. I studied up on the team. We talked about NDSU often, and he would share many great things about his favorite team. I learned how friends and family would travel annually to Frisco, Texas, for the national championship game. I learned that his brother was so confident in the NDSU program that he would buy tickets to the next national championship game before the season even began. He then began to trust me enough to share some of his business goals. That led to a more natural conversation about the problems our company solves and how we could solve them for him as well—all because of the interest I showed in something of personal importance to him. I would never have succeeded with him if I had only talked about my goals or what was important to me when we spoke.

In my experience, I've found this to be true of every elite seller I've met. They focus on their customer, and their interactions centered on what is best for the customer. I call this "living the Golden Rule" and choosing that mindset—always looking for opportunities to make someone else feel better or seek ways to make their life less difficult. Commonality and rapport make the sales process much more comfortable; they build trust, which alleviates the awkwardness of selling. The confidence you want to earn as a seller is not built through one phone call or in-person meeting. It's built over days, months, and years.

Trust is key in building relationships with your colleagues. A colleague recently shared with me the positive impact of an interaction we had years before. Each of us has been the new kid before, either at school or our first day on a job. It often fills us with anxiety: meeting new people, trying to earn their respect, and doing everything you can to not make a mistake. My colleague told me how surprised he was in the confidence I had in him so early in his career. He was so nervous the first time he had to interact with one of our customers. Although my relationship with my colleague was new, I trusted him and wanted to instill confidence in him.

I explained to our customer that they would hear directly from my colleague regarding the communication for this project and he would be driving the conversation. I would be copied on all correspondence, but I wanted them to know what to expect. This filled my colleague with the confidence that he would do a great job. I could have easily been more concerned with my reputation with our customer and my status as our number-one sales rep, but by showing genuine interest in my colleague's success and demonstrating real trust, I helped him believe in himself. I focused on finding ways for us to build a genuine team based on trust. I treated my colleague the way I would want to be treated in a new situation. My actions also set expectations with my customer, showing them that there was more than just *Casey* to help them. He had a team to depend on.

Earning Trust Takes A Huge Dose Of Patience

During my professional career, I worked with many amazing customers, but one stands out in particular—not only because of the time it took for me to win her trust, but also for the feeling I had when she gave me almost 90 percent of her business. She was one of my most loyal and longstanding customers. She was a vice president with five or so managers who reported to her. All of her managers hired consultants, which meant they were excellent business contacts for my company. Her organization utilized a complex system which generated problems which affected her human capital strategies. We had valuable solutions to those problems that could impact employee output toward her project roadmap.

My customer was one of the clients you get a little nervous approaching. She wasn't the tallest, but she was fierce and had a look in her eye that said she could easily body slam a salesperson, especially, if you were not going to immediately ask great questions and show her value. As I would find out later in our professional relationship, she was as genuine and loyal as they come, but you had to prove yourself to her first. Thankfully, I did.

Earlier on, when I had nothing in common with my customer, I tried to call her a few times with no luck. A year went by, and I tried again with no success. My pitch wasn't value based, and I was struggling to find rapport or anything in common. After three years, I slowly made some traction with her and a couple of her managers. That NDSU football fan? He was one of the managers who reported to my customer. He became a strong advocate for me as I worked to get that first meeting with his boss. He sold on my behalf to his manager, which caught her attention. I built on that foundation, and I felt my confidence growing in my approach with her. But she still wasn't ready to meet with me. Another year went by, and my team and I had won a few more deals and built some momentum.

Here was an email I sent her (with confidential information anonymized):

Hi Mrs. Customer,

My name is Casey Jacox, and I wanted to thank you for the opportunity to support your organization. As you may know, we are providing consulting services to Managers A, B, and C, which are genuinely helping to grow and launch product A. The feedback from your team has been very humbling, and we are committed and excited about the opportunity to take our partnership to the next level. Additionally, my team supports your marketing partner internally, and we are receiving great reviews from the talent my team has provided your organization.

I would love to schedule a time to share some metrics on our performance, as well as ensure you have clarity regarding the outcomes we are delivering within your organization. Next week, I am available on Monday, 1–3 pm, and on Tuesday, 12–2 pm. At your convenience, please let me know which time will work best for you to carve out 30 minutes to meet with me.

Best regards,

Casey Jacox

I hit send and said a little prayer. After 20 anxious minutes, she responded by saying "Monday at 1 pm would work. Please send me a calendar invite."

Five years later, I finally got the meeting!

The hard work had just started. It was time to elevate my skill set and make sure I was fully prepared for this meeting. It was just like Eminem's rap in "Lose Yourself" when he asks whether you'd take the opportunity to get everything you want or just let it slip away.

This moment is what separates the good salespeople from the bad. I knew I couldn't bullshit her; I had to be concise with my questions and answers. Who wouldn't take this opportunity and be prepared? Who wouldn't practice what they would say? When I chose to do those things, I was freed to be my authentic, genuine self. When I can be authentic, the customer can be at ease, and it's much easier to find the commonality and build the rapport that will lead to trust!

The meeting went very well. Judging by her body language, I could tell that she was impressed with the questions I asked, and with the value we were driving into her organization. She would go on to be one of my most loyal customers for 13 years. She would spend millions of dollars annually and ultimately become one of my influential champions. She always sold on my behalf and went to bat to support me when internal hiccups arose during procurement.

Recently, I asked my customer what her perception of the Golden Rule was as it related to my activities with her. "One of the things I appreciated in our business relationship is that you listened, intending to fully understand the issue, concern or problem to be solved first," she told me. "You were always grounded in that [understanding] before you took action. This helped ensure that the actions taken would be appropriate or enabled you to be honest about limitations or constraints that prevented you from taking action. Demonstrating understanding allowed our communication to be open and honest and helped to build trust. It wasn't surface level or cursory understanding but genuine and authentic."

This is proof of the power of the Golden Rule. Customers like her are what make the journey of selling so worthwhile. It was so hard to earn her trust, but I knew that there was not a chance in hell that I would ever lose it.

Try This Exercise

Have you seen patience work in your career?

Write down the names of three to five customers that you showed patience while earning their trust. Can you do it? If so, great! If not, that's OK. It just means you've found a gap that you can focus on improving.

Remember, customers want to buy products or services at their pace. When they feel pressured, their natural defense mechanisms will go up, and you could lose the deal. Customers want their problems solved, and they want them solved by sellers who genuinely understand their business and their problem. They want to know that their salesperson is patient yet driven to produce results for them. They seek salespeople who can show metrics on the real value a company is providing them. As much as we might not want to admit this, we are always one deal away from our last sale unless we make the simple choice to treat customers the way we want to be treated.

The brilliant Maya Angelou could not speak louder to salespeople who want to be known for their ability to provide elite customer service. Salespeople want to stay top-of-mind when their customers think of their product or service, but can they do that if they aren't following the Golden Rule and acting in a genuine, authentic fashion? The answer is simple: they can't, and as a result, they'll never be successful.

> *"I've learned that people will forget what you said, people will forget what you did, but people will never forget how you made them feel."*
>
> -Maya Angelou-

You have control of your daily actions and must realize the personal accountability for those actions. The Golden Rule is timeless advice for building long-term, successful relationships in both your personal and professional life.

CHAPTER 2:

Always Set Proper Expectations.

For the last 20 years, I've had the opportunity to work with some truly elite salespeople and sales leaders. With their colleagues and customers, they were always transparent and set expectations appropriately. This ability requires strong communication skills, something all these salespeople had: they could have tough conversations, their tone was appropriate, and they did not procrastinate. The connection between expectations and communication is key for an elite salesperson because inconsistent communication makes customers lose confidence. They question the salesperson's motives and wonder what is happening. This does not inspire trust and forces the client to create expectations in their minds that you won't be able to meet. As a seller, I never wanted my customer to be unsure of when they will hear from me, or to be confused about when we will implement our solution. No matter what the circumstances are, setting expectations will increase the chance to gain your customer's respect.

Even in your personal life, setting expectations will strengthen your relationships. Let's say you tell a friend that you will meet them at the restaurant at 4:00 pm, but due to traffic, you won't get there until 4:20 pm. You think to yourself, "Well, I'm only 20 minutes late, it's not that big of a deal," and you don't let them know you're going to be late. Meanwhile, your friend keeps looking at his or her watch, wondering where you are. Your friend might think you don't have any respect for them or their time. You will begin to erode their interest in spending time with you. It's the same thing with our customers, only magnified. Our friends might tolerate a little disrespect, but our customers won't. If you let your friend know you'll be late, you give them 20 minutes of their time back. It's a simple but effective way to gain respect. *Why?* Because you correctly set their expectations and eliminated negative thoughts or feelings about you. By over-communicating what your customers can expect, you increase your chances of creating winning relationships.

The ability to properly set expectations takes time and experience. I learned this skill by failing to set expectations. I took my customers' patience for granted in an early job as a barcode salesperson, and it bit me. I did not update them on the product ship date, so they became frustrated and impatient and then took their business elsewhere. Ouch, what a tough lesson for me to learn. I'd see sellers who kept their customers by keeping them abreast of everything. Had I simply communicated this change, the outcome of keeping a customer could've been different.

Setting expectations also aligns well with what you learned in Chapter 1 – Always embrace the Golden Rule.

Put yourself in your customer's shoes. Ask yourself, "How would I want to be treated? What do I need to know from my seller and why?" If you're unsure whether you should share information with the customer, be vulnerable enough to ask a colleague or your manager for advice. Instead of guessing how much to share with the customer and when, ask customers how often they want to hear from you, and what information they need. It sounds simple, but I find it's an advantage because your competitors aren't asking these questions. Take the guessing out of what you should do and allow your customers to drive the communication.

Setting expectations requires the confidence to do the right thing, even when it's not beneficial to you or your company. For example, at times, I would receive a phone call from a customer asking me to provide a service that was outside of our normal offering. *Here lies the lesson and choice I had to make.* Do I try to convince myself that we can help them? Or, do I do what is right: set their expectations properly and let them know that our firm doesn't provide that service. I am living proof that when you communicate this type of news to your customer, you will surprise them and differentiate yourself. You were honest, followed the Golden Rule and set expectations properly. This might seem simple, but it is not commonly practiced.

Unfortunately, some of us are not wired to think of others first. That is not always a bad thing; it's just human nature, but something that we all should be aware of when we think of ourselves instead of our customers. Being honest about how long it takes to deliver a solution or product is vital to winning relationships.

Early in my career, I found that even when my confidence wasn't the highest or my sales numbers weren't the best, I had to stay true to my values. If I did the right thing and properly set expectations with a customer, in the end, I would win. As I developed into an elite seller, my ability to set expectations with customers and internal teammates grew. I practiced in my personal life as well and found that these relationships began to improve. If you find yourself wanting to tell the customer what they want to hear, you are putting yourself and your company at risk of not being able to deliver. Being honest and upfront might lose you a sale in the short term, but it can build your reputation and trust with the customer over the long term, giving the customer a reason to recommend you or purchase from you another time.

In the middle of my career, I wanted to win a particular deal with a customer. When he finally called to say he wanted to meet and share the opportunity with me, I found it difficult to hide my enthusiasm. I understood what he wanted as we discussed his business and technical requirements. He then went on to share with me that we needed this work done in eight weeks and at a lower budget than I knew we could deliver.

Let me paint the picture of what was now going on inside of my head.

Imagine a cartoon where the devil pops up in a cloud off one shoulder and an angel pops up over the other shoulder. I could hear the devil on my shoulder say, "Just tell him yes and get the business." Then I heard the angel say, "There is no way you can meet the timeframe needed with his budgetary requirements." The angel was right, and I knew it. When I followed up with my customer, I explained that I was thankful for the opportunity but that I would need to pass. He was in shock, almost to the point of being upset. I explained that I had worked so hard to finally get in front of him and potentially earn his business, but I knew we couldn't do what he was asking, and I didn't want to hurt his hard-earned trust in me. He was blown away and thanked me for my honesty. He went on to say how refreshing it was to work with a company (and a salesperson) that wasn't afraid to walk away from business because they knew they couldn't deliver. This was a defining moment, and it's as clear today as it was then.

Try This Exercise

Time to break out your journal again. Think back to a time when you didn't correctly set expectations. What was the negative impact or outcome to you, your company, or your customer? If you could do it again, what would you do differently? Write down two or three lessons you learned through this experience.

The Importance Of Communication

Refining how you communicate is just as important as what you communicate when setting expectations. The tone of your voice in both spoken conversations and writing creates an emotional reaction in your audience; it can build confidence, fear, or even confusion about your message.

Let me give you an example. As a college quarterback at Central Washington University, I steadily built relationships with my teammates. This was accomplished during many off-season workouts; however, the in-depth relationships were built during actual games. When I went into a huddle and called a play, I needed to have a confident tone so my teammates would trust that I knew what I was doing. If I called the play with a shaking voice and I didn't look my teammates in the eye, they wouldn't trust me, and they probably wouldn't perform at their best. The role of a quarterback is to instill confidence in the play and make your teammates believe that anything is possible. You work together to achieve a common goal.

The same holds true with your customers. Change is always happening, and most of the time, we have zero control over the potential outcomes. What we can control is the confidence in our voice and how clearly we articulate expectations to our customer, whether negative or positive. Being realistic with your customers throughout your sales process will save them from being surprised. Customers never want to be surprised with unplanned news regarding their service. I've found that when you aren't ahead of communication to your customer, you open the door for a competitor to expand their footprint and erode your client relationship. Additionally, an optimistic tone in your voice can also inspire confidence and trust, which will be important when problems arise.

As sellers on the path to becoming elite, we must be ready to anticipate potential problems. Challenges will always exist. We can deal with them negatively and hurt our customers' trust or take the opportunity to deal with that change in a positive, transparent manner, which will always increase confidence.

Tone of communication isn't the only important aspect of setting expectations. It is also important to communicate in a timely manner—don't put it off! The million-dollar question we ask ourselves as sellers is, "According to research done by Hubspot, 51 percent want salespeople to respond in a timely manner[3]." We've all had to realize that time is money. As sellers, if we're going to win more relationships, we must think about ways to save our customers time and deliver value. Not getting back to our customers will only increase our chances of losing the deal or hurting a relationship—and so will showing up late for an appointment. When meeting with a customer, my goal was to always show up 15 minutes early for a meeting. This was my definition of being on time. When I accomplished that goal, I could relax and ensure I was fully engaged and prepared to have a great meeting. I was ready to ask thought provoking questions that would make me memorable to my customer. Alternatively, if you come in hot at 85 mph in the parking lot, skid out, accidentally park in the handicap spot with sweat coming down your face, ask yourself, "are you now in a good spot to have a productive meeting? "This should be an easy question for you to answer. Obviously, no!

Real World Customer Example

Sometimes the expectation has to be modified to a greater degree. Throughout my career, sales leaders would advise me that I needed to act like a chameleon. Meaning, you must be able to think on your feet and work with many different types of personalities. You may need all of your communication skills to accomplish this in a way that creates a winning situation for everyone.

At a later stage of my career, I was presented with an amazing opportunity. One of our customers was responsible for the customer facing division of one of the world's largest wireless and media companies.

One of our key relationships was with a vice president (VP) who had quickly become a champion for us, always seeking new ways to help us grow our business. At one point, she offered us a much larger project, which meant we would replace a firm known for more value-based, consultative services. Since our brand was more traditionally staffing centric, I had to work hard to prove that my team could deliver and truly compete with these larger consulting firms, based upon market perception. After roughly nine months of multiple stakeholder meetings and negotiations, we were awarded the deal which felt like we won the gold medal at the Olympics.

One of my favorite memories of winning this deal actually involved a practical joke that I played on our CEO. We had scheduled a call to provide him the news of this historic win and let him know that the deal was only going to happen if we would install a mechanical bull inside of our Dallas office. It took every ounce of sarcasm to pull this off before I told him I was joking, and the deal was ours!

The deal involved hiring 70–90 consultants with unique, in-demand skills that would allow us to meet our customer's deliverables and timeline.

Sometime later, we had a series of meetings with the customer, including the VP who had provided the opportunity initially. The sessions were going very well. We were getting rave reviews about our performance, and our executive team couldn't have been happier with my team's performance.

Our last meeting of the day was with the financial sponsor. She was a seasoned professional who displayed confidence that could easily intimidate you if you weren't on you're a "A" game.

As our meeting was ending, she said, "I sure hope that I can find some money for this project."

I replied, "That's funny. Good one."

"I'm not joking," she said. "We have budget issues."

GULP! This was almost a change your underwear moment.

The VP explained that there was a lot of project consolidation happening, which would affect our project, including our newly hired team of 50-plus consultants.

After the meeting, our team met internally and agreed that we saw some challenges ahead. My CEO asked that I keep everyone in the loop so we could keep expectations clear. For the next few weeks, I would send a recap to our executive team to make sure they knew of any financial risk or budget cuts. By choosing to keep everyone in the loop and communicating frankly and promptly, I eliminated surprise. We knew bad news was looming. I didn't want anyone in my company to be blindsided.

Three months later, as I was preparing for a sales performance trip, the phone rang. It was the VP who oversaw the project. She said, "We are in trouble, and I am so sorry." I took a deep breath, actively listened, and told her I understood her business challenge. She then said, "We lost 70 percent of our budget, and we need to eliminate roughly 50–55 of your consultants within three weeks." Showing empathy in that moment, proved I was there to support her through this difficult time. Not only was this a huge hit for our company, but a very painful experience she had to go through as well given the impact this had on her staff.

Remarkably, I stayed calm while talking to her, but inside I was anxious about making the right decision. Given my upcoming trip, I would have only two weeks to devise a plan and break the bad news to the consultants who would be losing their jobs. I had to share the news not only with my team, but also with my executives so that everyone understood our potential financial risk.

The best thing I could do was set proper expectations by being honest. Once I realized this was my only responsible option, the anxiety went away. *As I look back, this is the power of setting proper expectations for my team.*

Keeping this information inside my head would only make things worse and create unnecessary anxiety. It might seem easier to keep this information to myself and pretend the bad news wasn't happening, but I knew I couldn't. As you probably can relate, procrastinating always increases stress and frustration—for you and those impacted by the procrastination. The problem wasn't going away, and

I had to respond with confidence, both internally and externally.

As I began to tackle this difficult road head on, I chose to lean on my teammates and my leaders for support. First, I sent a very detailed email to all the leaders in our firm who would feel the financial impacts. I could've easily delegated this task to my fellow sales team or recruiting staff, but I knew this was my responsibility. I then met with my teammates and our consultants and explained the difficult situation that we faced. I shared with them that this was not their fault, nor ours. The only option was for our consultants to quickly update their résumés so we could re-deploy them at one of our other clients as soon as possible. While some people were very angry and disappointed, the majority appreciated my willingness to lead from the front and face the problem. The choice I made to set expectations not only reduced frustration, but it also gave my team confidence to work with the affected consultants. As a team, we would end up redeploying nearly 75 percent of them to other customers and keep them working on exciting, impactful projects.

This business experience was one of the most challenging days of my career. I had been responsible for winning the largest deal in my company's history, which, became one of the most significant project failures.

After the dust had settled, I met with my customer and she said something that still greatly impacted me positively to this day:

> *"Casey, I can't thank you and your team enough for how you've handled this situation. The day you won this, you were Casey, and as I look at you today, with all of this adversity, you are still Casey. I want you to know how much I appreciate that, and that is why you will have my trust for life."*

That, by far, was one of the most humbling moments of my life. As I shared with you in Chapter 1, I made a choice to treat both my customer and my team the way I wanted to be treated. By making this choice, I communicated as soon as changes became known, and doing that adjusted everyone's expectations. If I hadn't done either of those, the outcome would have been very different. Had I kept the news to myself, I would surely have damaged the relationship with my internal team, as well as my executive team.

How could they trust I was being truthful if I was capable of holding back information like this? More importantly, I would have lost a customer by choosing to blame them for the problem. My customer told me I had her trust precisely because I had been honest and set expectations appropriately.

My reaction was also about giving my customer the benefit of the doubt. I reminded myself that this is the last thing my customer wanted to deal with. I told myself, "Do you think she woke up wishing they would lose the budget and couldn't wait to tell me the bad news?" Of course, she didn't! And that's why I wanted to make an uncomfortable situation as comfortable as I could and show empathy.

Setting proper expectations and communicating clearly paid off well for us. Two years later, my team had become this customer's top vendor by outperforming and out servicing our competitors. After the turbulence had passed, my client began to regain her budget. She continued to bring exclusive business my way, mainly because of how I had responded to the crisis. My team also learned the positive impacts of proper communication in a time when it would have been easy to choose the wrong path.

As I look back at how difficult this experience was, I am now thankful for the lessons learned, as well the opportunities to provide leadership to my customer and my colleagues.

CHAPTER 3:

Don't Just Hear Your Customers, Listen To Them.

Salespeople are taught to listen to customer problems, diagnose their needs, and then provide a meaningful solution. That sounds so easy, doesn't it? Yet, not commonly practiced. There is a difference between hearing someone and listening to them, and we'll discuss the difference in a moment.

A salesperson lacking the ability to listen is one of the biggest reason's customers dislike salespeople. But it goes beyond just dislike. Did you know that according to CrowdRiff content manager Julia Manoukian, "only 18 percent of customers trust salespeople."[4] Essentially what that says is that if you have 100 customers, only 18 of them actually believe what you are saying! How scary is that?

The optimist in me knows that this is a great opportunity. Listening is a skill, which means it can only be improved through consistent practice. The best listeners I've ever known took a genuine interest in other people. They also maintained excellent eye contact during a conversation and wouldn't allow for outside forces to distract them, such as a cell phone or smart watch notification. When a customer sees your authentic self, they will begin to realize that you care about them, and you will see trust start to form. Remember what Mike Robbins taught us before in the chapter 1? "Be yourself, everyone else is already taken."

Real listening shows that you care. As Mark Roberge, SVP of sales at Hubspot, says[5]:

> *"You know you are running a modern sales team when selling feels more like the relationship between a doctor and a patient and less like a relationship between a salesperson and a prospect. It's no longer about interrupting, pitching and closing. It is about listening, diagnosing and prescribing."*

Towards the end of my sales career, I was selected to join a small team tasked with training over 800 salespeople on a new, value-based methodology. This project required us to truly listen to what our customers were telling us. We interviewed them to understand what they believed we did well and then used that data to craft and refine our message. Just building the training content for our sales teams took more than a year and required many days and nights away from my family.

One of the critical elements of this transformation focused on asking our salespeople a fundamental question: "What problems do you solve for your customers?" That seems easy, until you get different personalities and levels of experience trying to answer this question. What I found through this journey, is that different interpretations of a company's value-add are common inside of large organizations who've been in business for years.

People hear information through the filter of their perceptions, which drives their reality. In this situation, perception drove what our salespeople believed we were providing for our customers.

As the sales transformation went on, it became more apparent that our message needed to be polished and consistent across all markets. When customers lose confidence in salespeople and the companies they do business with, nothing good will come from that experience unless you make changes for the better. When customer confusion occurs, companies lack clarity about understanding and solving customer problems and show they aren't truly listening to their customers.

Influential facilitator, John Kaplan, calls this "Seller Deficit Disorder."[6] The disorder has two key symptoms found in why customers don't trust salespeople:

1. **They believe salespeople don't understand their business.**
2. **They believe salespeople don't listen.**

Ask yourself this question—and be honest: How often have you committed the cardinal sin of selling by not listening to your customer? How many examples can you think of where you could have handled that situation differently?

Every salesperson is guilty of this sometimes in their career; even the most elite don't listen well from time to time. We all have excuses on why we don't always listen. For example, we get so excited to make our point that we think the customer must hear from us right away. Or, there's too much pressure to make outbound phone calls, or there's not enough time to research the prospective customer. I get it. I've been there. But you have to stop making excuses. Once I stopped making those excuses, I became a much more of an effective listener. If you become self-aware and take action to drive positive behaviors, your customer will notice it immediately. This is one additional key element for you to stay on the path to winning more relationships.

Hearing vs. Listening

Hearing and listening are not the same. When we make a conscious choice between them, we alter our pursuit to build long-term relationships.

Over my 20 years of business experience, I've seen relationships ruined by a lack of listening as key information was missed by someone during a conversation or meeting. When people aren't listening, they are only hearing sounds and subconsciously letting other information go in one ear and out the other. The brutal truth of only hearing someone is that your customer, friend, or spouse can feel that ingenuine behavior. Listening requires your full attention. Turn off notifications on your device, put down your phone, close your computer and look someone directly in the eye. This is how you make the other person feel like they have your undivided attention.

As I thought more about the differences between hearing and listening, it resonated that a visual aid would help tell the story. On the next page, you will see a chart outlining these differences.

	HEARING	**LISTENING**
What is the difference?	Hearing is an ability.	Listening is a skill that you can practice.
What is involved in hearing vs. listening?	Hearing only uses your ears without a conscious focus. Poor body language will be felt by the person you're speaking with.	Listening uses your mind! It is a psychological skill that is learned through practice. Active body language will show you are engaged and present.
What are the different outcomes?	You will lose customers, friends, and relationships by only hearing what is said.	You will win more relationships by listening and retaining key information.

Try This Exercise

Review this table, analyze the differences and <u>write down</u> what resonates most with you. What memories or interactions with customers or internal associates come to mind? How did these thoughts make you feel? What did you regret? What would you have done differently?

Whether you're a salesperson or a sales leader, take time to review this chart with your sales team. Talk about the key differences together and seek areas where you might be falling short in your daily opportunities to build relationships. You will be surprised by what you learn from your teammates through this exercise.

What resonated most for me was the fact that hearing is an innate ability, while listening is a skill. Listening is the skill of retaining information, whereas hearing is just obtaining noise without processing the message or acting on it. A skill is learned, which means that when we practice listening, we can increase our ability to have more positive, outcome-based conversations.

If we find ourselves thinking we are listening when we are only hearing, we put our companies and ourselves at risk of losing relationships. Hubspot asked customers what they want from sales professionals, and 69 percent said, "Listen to my needs."[7]   Notice that they didn't say "Hear my needs." They didn't say, "Let information go in one ear and out the other." They didn't say, "Nod your head and pretend to listen." And they definitely didn't say, "Look at your smart watch or smartphone during the conversation." These distractions happen to all of us, but we need to be mindful and curtail our behavior. Customers are begging salespeople to listen.

Ways To Listen

One way to listen rather than hear is to cultivate a genuine interest in your customer and their business problem. Many of my customers tell me that they've always loved my curiosity. They knew I cared. My body language proved my genuine interest in them; I made solid eye contact and was never distracted. While you might have innate curiosity, it can also be a learned skill. Think about great listeners in your life. I'd be willing to bet they asked great, thought-provoking questions. These questions are the ones that propel conversations to new levels of communication.

"Asking questions about your buyer's goals and pain points leads to better sales success." —Gong[8]

Great questions are an easy way for you to leave your mark on a customer. To prepare for a meeting, research your customer and their company. Doing so will prompt questions you can ask to show your customer your interest in them. In today's impatient world, too many sellers choose to wing it. They ask a wide variety of questions that sometimes won't have a flow and usually end up confusing your customer.

Be someone who shows thought-provoking curiosity in a related way, as it will surely impress a customer and show them that you cared enough to do your homework before the meeting.

Another way to ensure that you are listening rather than just hearing is to be confident. Inexperienced sales reps tend to lack confidence and worry more about what they should say rather than listening first in order to diagnose the customer's problem.

As we learned in Chapter 1, vulnerability is a crucial skill in treating others the way you want to be treated. Vulnerability is also a critical skill in listening because listening means you might not have a response right away. You have to be willing to say, "I don't know." Be honest with the customer and acknowledge when you're not familiar with a word, phrase, or subject or don't have a ready answer. Let them know you will do some research and get back to them with a response. This approach demonstrates that you will work to understand your customer and see things from their standpoint.

You'll have more sincere discussions by going into a conversation without any expectations—and that builds real, longstanding relationships. By showing vulnerability, everyone can improve.

Next time your customer shares their problem with you, really listen and don't be afraid to say, "I don't know or I'm not sure, could you describe that in more detail?" when you might not understand something they are explaining to you.

A third way to listen rather than hear is to "seek to understand before you seek to be understood," another of Covey's *7 Habits*. I encountered this example during my life while calling a technical support line. I kept explaining my issue, but the tech support professional on the other side of the phone kept answering questions I hadn't asked. He was more focused on his training materials and what he was supposed to say than on trying to understand my problem. His lack of self-awareness quickly turned me off. Not only was he sharing information that wasn't relevant or useful, but he also wasn't answering my questions or helping solve my problem. Due to this poor experience, I chose to take my business elsewhere.

Unfortunately, these uncomfortable and avoidable conversations still happen in every industry, not just tech support. Hopefully, one of these days, companies will make it a priority to measure success and hold their sellers accountable for consistent training needed to handle these customer interactions.

It can be hard for some salespeople to seek to understand a customer challenge, but by refocusing on your customer's problem through asking open-ended questions, one can honestly assess whether you can help them or not. Once you can sincerely understand what your customer is sharing with you, your responses will also change and improve the quality of relationships you're building. Asking the right questions will benefit the customer and help you transform the relationship.

According to Chorus, "The top reps [are] up to **10 times more likely** to use collaborative language [words like us, we, and our] than low-performing reps."[9] Low performers, by contrast, use "factional language": words that distance the salesperson from the customer and de-emphasize empathy. For example, if a seller only uses words that describe what he or she wants to do or say, then they quickly will erode the chance of winning a relationship and turning them into a customer.

A consultative seller will show more curiosity, listen more, and talk less. Your actions show whether you are listening, and customers pick up on body language. When we are only hearing, we don't make eye contact, we stare at our phones, or we fiddle with objects near us. When you're on the receiving end, it can feel as though the person is staring right through you, which is awkward for both of you. Make a habit of looking people in the eye. Put away distractions so you can truly listen.

It's fine to take notes, of course, as long as you do it thoughtfully. I have to admit, I'm still old school and prefer to take handwritten notes when meeting with a customer. But whether you type or handwrite, always ask your customer if you can take notes in the meeting. Simple as that might sound, little gestures of respect like that can open up a more positive conversation. By getting approval to take notes, you set expectations that you might break eye contact in order to document the information accurately. As I gained more experience, I learned to write notes while looking the customer in the eye.

Those notes can open new, unexpected doors for you. For example, let's imagine you're meeting with Bob, and he shares with you that his peer, Susan, is having a similar problem, and he believes your product could help her as well. After your meeting, you ask for permission to use his name when following up with Susan. He gives you the green light, and you share with Susan that Bob mentioned her and thought your product could be of value regarding some of her current business problems. Susan agrees to meet with you, and you take the time to listen to her and make a sale. Congratulations! By really listening and taking good notes, you met another potential client.

A couple of additional points to keep in mind:

- **Always get permission to follow up on leads that were shared with you.** When you do, you execute lessons learned in Chapters 1-3, you show them that you care, and want the customer to lead you. Just because a customer mentions a peer in their organization, always ask for their approval to use their name when following up. I found that to be an impactful step in the relationship building process.

- **Once you meet with the person referred to you, don't assume you can help.** Even if it's your best customer doing the referring, you don't necessarily have all the answers to the prospect's problem. You still have to treat them like any new prospect and ensure they are telling you their problem versus you assuming you already know everything.

     Early in my career, I violated both of these points. I assumed I could help a customer without genuinely seeking to understand their problem. I didn't ask great questions, and I didn't actively listen. As a result, not only did I embarrass myself, but I also ended up losing a business contact I was pursuing to build a relationship with. It frustrates me to this day, even though my mistake happened nearly 18 years ago. I vowed that my communication would never be so unclear again. My unfortunate story has become a great lesson to share with many of the sales reps I coached, trained, and mentored.

Impact Of Not Listening

You might be asking yourself if all of this really matters? Well, it does. You must not take this lesson lightly if you have goals of becoming elite and winning more relationships. The effect of not listening to the real issue can be catastrophic to a relationship if mishandled.

Too often throughout my career, I saw a leader's or salesperson's ego getting in the way of decision-making. They might have started to listen, but then they fell into the habit of only hearing, which would frustrate the customer, ultimately damaging the relationship. The individual would focus solely on being right rather than solving the customer's problem. One of my former executives earlier in my career, would always counsel me, **"You can be right, or you can get what you want."** What you want is for the customer to be happy so that you can win the relationship. When we only hear someone, we run the risk of missing information and only focusing on being right – which will only increase our chances of losing the relationship.

This problem can happen within a company when employees deal with each other. Think about the last time you and one of your colleagues argued. Were you arguing because you were hearing each other rather than listening to each other?

I've seen this scenario play out frequently between the marketing and finance departments. They don't take time to ask questions and seek to understand the other department's viewpoint. Instead, they dig their heels in and refuse to budge. They know they are right—at least from their perspective. But this ego-centric communication only erodes any hope of teamwork, resulting in unplanned employee turnover. Even worse, this behavior can impact the customer, because when this dynamic occurs internally, people think it's acceptable. Not so. I take you back to Chapter 1 as we seek to win relationships and not just deals.

By intently focusing on listening, you will find it much easier to communicate and add value to the conversation. If you want to drive this point home with your sales team, ask your sellers to watch the hilarious scene with the slimy car salesman from National Lampoon's *Vacation* (1983).[10] Chevy Chase's character plays the role of Clark W. Griswold and goes to the car dealership looking to bring home the brand new family station wagon. There, Clark has an encounter with the salesperson named Ed, played by the funny and talented Eugene Levy. Throughout this scene, Ed only hears but does not listen. Not only does he lack self-awareness and listening skills, but he calls Clark Griswold's son by the wrong name. "How you doing? Reuben, right?" "No, it's Rusty," Clark's son corrects him. As you watch, you will see how he tries to close a deal rather than win a relationship. Griswold clearly stated that he was looking for an Antarctic blue sports wagon for the family to take across country to Wally World, but what's ready for him is a metallic pea "family truckster." Ed tries to hardcore-sell Clark the truckster, while the old family car is being crushed in the background of the movie scene. Not only did Ed not listen to his customer, but he also didn't set proper expectations because the car Clark wanted wasn't even on the lot! Behavior like Ed's gives salespeople a bad name. As funny as it may seem, this happens too often with sellers and customers.

Remember that we were all created with two ears and one mouth for a reason: do more listening than talking. No matter what the situation might be, focus on truly listening. Let the other person finish their point and provide them the opportunity to ask their question *before* you respond.

Try This Exercise

For the next two weeks, I challenge you and your team to focus specifically on active listening. Whoever your audience is, do not interrupt. Let them finish. When they ask you a question, ensure that you respond with the answer to *that* question. After two weeks, talk as a team and share your best practices. What worked particularly well for you?

This will help create a culture of listening and learning—one that your customers will thank you for.

CHAPTER 4:

Always Document And Follow Up.

When it comes to winning relationships, documentation and follow-up will help make you memorable. Any notes from a meeting you write down through an interaction with a customer counts as documentation. Those notes help you retain the information the customer shares with you.

The activities you do to connect with the customer after a meeting are the follow-up steps. According to *Marketing Donut*, the majority of all B2B (business to business) sales require five follow-ups. It also found that 44 percent of salespeople give up after one rejection, 22 percent give up after two rejections, 14 percent give up after three, 12 percent after four, and only 8 percent follow up five times. [11]

To win more relationships, you must make following up extremely important and ensure that you don't allow your competition to take the clients you're striving to win. Meaning, if your customer tells you and your competitor to follow up on a specific date and you forget, guess what happens? Your competitor remembered and now he or she just showed your target customer that you didn't listen and follow up as well as they did.

Moreover, if you don't follow up when there is a problem, you definitely will lose the relationship. Customers want to work with true professionals. They want to work with salespeople who will effectively communicate the good, the bad, and the ugly. If your customer shares with you that they are experiencing a challenge with their business and they ask you to follow up in two weeks, you have a simple choice: Follow up, or don't. When I had these situations occur during my selling career, I would always follow up and remind the customer that I was doing so at their request. For example, if my customer "Todd" asked me to call on January 18th, then I would. My initial response to him would be, "Hi Todd, I wanted to follow up with you per your advice from our last correspondence, is now a good time for us to speak?" This shows that I listened and followed through.

It's easy to be the seller who only shares good news, but remember, customers will respect you more for telling them the bad news upfront. As we work to win relationships with our customers or colleagues, we have the opportunity to show our real character. We can respond in a positive way when faced with difficult business challenges.

Try This Exercise

Look back to a time when you were tasked to follow up and share bad news. How did you do it? What was the result, and how did it impact your relationship? What would you do differently now that you can look back at the outcome? How did the power of documenting help you or hurt you as you analyze your personal example?

One question you might be asking yourself - what should you be documenting in a customer meeting? How much information is too much and how little is too little? Stop thinking so much about what you *think* your customer needs and listen to what they're actually telling you. When they share information about their personal or professional lives, *document it*. When you hear your customer is heading to their son's lacrosse game, document it. If you hear they're attending their daughter's band concert, document it. Those are nuggets of information you can use to establish commonality and rapport with your customer. In the end, you will always need to articulate your value and ensure you solve a business problem for your customer. But doing the little things to make your customer feel heard, will separate you from the rest.

Documentation Avenues

All sellers have the same number of minutes in a day: 1,440. I realized that if I wanted to get ahead in my career and win more relationships, I needed to become more efficient than my competitors. Becoming more efficient meant that I needed to evaluate all of the tools that were at my disposal to generate more relationships.

According to an article on LinkedIn, "75 percent to 85 percent of the top salespeople value CRM's, productivity apps, email marketing, and social selling as key factors in their success."[12]. That resounding stat clarifies what it takes to become an elite salesperson.

To effectively win relationships, you first must document what you heard and enter that data into your customer relationship management (CRM) system. The information you capture will document and continue to drive the sales process, as will utilizing the information you hear to organically create commonality and rapport. Applying what you hear and documenting it will help you save countless hours as a salesperson.

One of the biggest mistakes I see salespeople make is treating the documentation process as a waste of time. According to CSO Insights, "the percentage of salespeople attaining quota is decreasing year over year: from 63 percent in 2012 to 53 percent in this year's study."[13] Those reps surely are not documenting and following up with their customers. If you aren't tracking what your customer shared with you, how can you follow up five times to win the relationship? CRM systems are a great way to do this.

Whenever I heard colleagues complain about the time it takes to document, (internally) I would shake my head in frustration as they didn't see the value this system would provide them. Surely, our investment in seeking long-term relationships is worth the effort to document. One day I couldn't stay quiet anymore and had to speak up with a younger associate.

My company had an annual President's Club trip for the top sales associates and revenue support teams. During a networking breakout, one of my colleagues complimented me on my success within our firm. He asked, "What are some things I can work on to improve my skill set?" I asked him a few questions to find out where some of his struggles might be. It turned out his struggle was a lack of documentation in our CRM system. He did not have the daily discipline of documenting his conversations and meetings. I asked him what his current book of business looked like in terms of run rate (revenue and profit). He responded, "Oh, it's been a great year!" and gave me a number. I quickly did the math and realized that my year-end revenue and gross profit numbers were four times as much as his were. I asked if he knew that our company could run usage reports on our CRM to see who was using it and to what extent. He didn't. I then asked if he knew my current numbers. Again, he didn't. I shared my current sales production with him, and his eyes widened. He said, "Really, wow – that is really impressive?" Given that information, he didn't think my CRM usage rankings could be very high. What I did next was a great teaching moment that I don't think my associate will ever forget. I looked him straight in the eye and said, "I'm currently #1 in overall production in our CRM and #1 in sales production firm-wide."

It wasn't an accident that these numbers aligned. I used the CRM system to work more efficiently. I was able to demonstrate to my associate that the problem wasn't the system, the problem was himself. He had been making excuses about why he couldn't adapt to the CRM instead of asking for help and looking for ways to become efficient.

After the trip, I taught him my best practices to be more efficient and productive. Once he implemented them, he started to see dramatic increases in his sales numbers, which continued for years to come. He continued to thank me over the years and it was always enjoyable to hear about his progress. I would tell him that I appreciated his kind words, but now it was his turn to share the message of learning with others in our firm. By sending the elevator back down, he would mentor others who could learn from his mistake and dramatically increase their sales best practices.

Documenting in your CRM isn't enough, however. You have to let the system help you manage your day. Too often in my career, I would see salespeople choosing to use siloed documentation tools, such as plain paper, notes on their phone, and spreadsheets. When these sellers would choose to document in this manner, not many positive outcomes would be generated. Their information was scattered, and they didn't always remember to check all those tools. Whenever you record what you've learned in your CRM, all your information will be in one place, and you'll be able to set a reminder of when and why to follow up with a potential customer. I used to joke that adequately using a CRM for follow-up reminders allowed me to look much smarter than I was. It honestly took the guessing out of who I should call on any given day and why.

Before I learned to document and follow up, my failures were a painful reminder of why it was necessary. Any time I was late following up with a customer who told me when to call, I would feel embarrassed and, more importantly, I was frustrated that I had missed an opportunity to win a relationship. Not only did I lose the relationship by not following up, but I lost the deal. I made the wrong choice due to my own lack of organizational skills and put myself in the mediocre salesperson bucket. It was awful! I finally learned how to let the software help me remember when to follow up, and it's led to many more customers and relationships won over time. More importantly, it has led to deeper customer interactions and meaningful, long-lasting relationships.

Try This Exercise

I want you to think about this for a minute. Imagine a day where you come into the office and log into your CRM. There are your calls, meetings and tasks already scheduled y for you. How would that make you feel? Write down 2-3 words that come to mind.

Would you feel more organized? Better prepared to win those relationships? You can turn this vision into a reality if you choose daily to use your CRM to drive your activity. It requires discipline, no doubt, but it does pay off. Always have a follow-up activity open for all of your sales prospects. If you don't, then why would you put them in your CRM in the first place? Seems like an easy answer to me and hopefully you as well.

Not only will proper documentation and follow-up help you win more relationships, but it will also help you retain your current customers. Propeller reports that "retaining current customers is six to seven times less costly than acquiring new ones."[14] But just because you are doing an excellent job for a customer today, doesn't mean they will always buy from you in the future.

Complacency is a killer for sales reps, and the stat above should motivate you to never take a customer for granted. They can leave at any time and we as sellers, must always do the little things to keep them happy. Your competition will always be trying to get in the door. If you follow the strategies in each chapter of this book, you will dramatically increase your chances of keeping and winning the relationship.

Let's see this in action. For example, let's say I met with a customer and they told me to follow up in three weeks when they might have more information to share with me. This is a pivotal moment in the sales process. If I choose to document this meeting in my CRM, I would note precisely what the customer told me: "follow up in three weeks, based upon the specific advice the customer shared with me." I would save that activity and then set a reminder inside of the CRM that would prompt me to call that customer at the future date he or she advised me. The follow-up conversation would sound like this, "Hi, Ms. Customer, during our last correspondence on May 15, you asked me to follow up with you in three weeks to better understand how we might work together." When I do that, I immediately gain my sales prospect's confidence by showing her that I followed up when I said I would. I built trust by reminding her what she told me to do. Tickletrain reports that "only 2 percent of sales transactions happen during a first meeting."[15] This all might sound very elementary; however, it is a step that most sellers skip. They get lazy and hope they remember who, when and why to call a customer. The stark reality is that you can't remember everything if you don't take time to document. That excellent stat further drives home the point of why proper documentation and follow-up are vital if you genuinely want to win people in the long term.

Creativity In Documentation

The life of a salesperson can be a grind. There is a constant challenge to grow your business, build new skill sets, and find creative ways to establish new customers. Sales calls or meetings can become routine if you allow them to. Elite sellers are always challenging themselves to grow each day, and they look at each interaction with a customer as an opportunity to separate themselves from their competition. If you allow complacency to set in, one follow-up can sound a lot like the next to the customer. When that happens, you can lose focus and let important things slip by.

Some of my family and friends became pilots for well-known airlines. As I began to educate myself on the planning and preparation they took for each flight, I started to see some similarities in the profession of becoming an elite seller. As I talked with these pilots, we realized the grind of selling can share similarities as an airline pilot, from a preparation and planning perspective. Before each flight, the captain or co-captain must go through a checklist. They must continuously check gauges and courses. They also communicate with the passengers during the flight, such as when they are about to hit turbulence. Now, pilots can fly up to 1,000 hours each year, so they get used to the routine of takeoff, landing, and everything in between. However, elite pilots treat each flight like it was their first flight and the passengers and crew can feel the difference. They can hear the professionalism in their voice. Would you be comfortable with a pilot like that? Of course you would! You know they're taking their duties seriously and taking care of you. Would you be so confident with a pilot who didn't tell you when you were about to hit major turbulence? Who didn't explain why you were being delayed? Who bounced the plane upon landing? I don't know about you, but I would stay clear of that flight!

To stay focused and be successful, I searched for ways to more effectively document and follow up. One straightforward yet effective method I used was to send a meeting recap email to the customer. This form of documentation was a simple way to drive more value out of my everyday follow-up. In the meeting recap, I would thank the customer for their time and outline exactly what I heard, using a story format. I would write in a conversational style, highlighting the problems or challenges they might be facing and then describe how my service could positively impact their business. I would end the recap by asking the customer to let me know if any of my notes or data were incorrect. By sending this kind of message, I showed the customer how committed I was to their business and that I actively listened during our meeting. The customer also had an opportunity to provide any new information that might have arisen since the meeting, such as new sales opportunities or challenges I might be able to address.

Below is an example of a meeting recap/follow-up email that I wrote to a customer (using fictional names, of course). For this customer, we had a large consultant workforce in and around her scope of responsibility. She could influence the work that could come our way, so this was a large follow-up letter that provided me the opportunity to move the relationship forward.

As you read this letter below, think about the strategies in each of the chapters I've shared so far. What did I ask for from the customer? Did my message clarify what I learned in my meeting with her? How so? What stood out to you? Next, compare this letter with your current follow-ups that you might be or not be doing. Are you doing any of the things I am here? In what ways are your letters different? Lastly, I want you to write about how you can improve your follow-up letters to win more relationships.

Veronica,

Thank you again for your time today. It was great to meet you and learn more about your business. Below is a recap of what we discussed today, so please let me know if any of my notes don't align with our conversation.

<u>What We Learned</u>

The new digital organization under Company A has been tasked with executing digital transformation and transforming the online channel while improving customer experience in three key areas:

- *Build capabilities that enable the customer lifecycle across all channels.*
- *Enable employees to deliver on customer expectations.*
- *Drive online and omnichannel sales and service capabilities that continue to deliver features and functionality.*

We heard that you recently went through another reorg that we believe is broken down in this fashion:

- *The business team focused on KPIs is now led by John Smith.*

- *The product team focused on capabilities is now led by Jane Brown.*
- *CX/UX are under Michelle Thompson, with Purcell Jefferson and Julie Wu reporting to her.*
- *Your team, portfolio strategy, and operations will manage deliverables, funding, and ROI, as well as Agile execution, omnichannel, communications, and customer loyalty.*
- *Additionally, Agile/SAFe execution has been a big push, having some successes and struggles but overall finding a happy medium so far.*

Next Steps And Action Items

You've agreed to offer a warm introduction to your three vendor managers (NY based) so that my colleague, Travis and I can get acquainted with them and provide our customer journey map (story) and how we have supported Company A over the last 18 years. The goal of these introductions will allow me to introduce two of my teammates to begin building new relationships with your team when they travel to NYC next month.

I will also schedule reoccurring monthly calls with you to ensure we keep lines of communication open
and that we stay abreast of current business challenges that might offer opportunities for us to
work together.

Thanks again for your time. Please let me know if I've missed anything or if you have any additional questions.

Best regards,

Casey Jacox

Multiple Sales Reps In A Meeting —Documentation Best Practices

So far, we've covered the core ways to follow up with your clients and how documentation can provide such a positive impact to you and your business. What happens when you and your team are meeting together with a customer? How do you know that you all heard the same thing from the customer? What processes do you have in place to ensure your team isn't going in opposite directions and the appropriate information was captured?

In the staffing and consulting industry, communication was crucial to ensure that we all heard the same thing. If we didn't double-check with each other and have a proper debrief, we would find ourselves in a world of hurt. We would be working hard but not smart, and we would eventually upset our customers by providing consultants who could not meet their business needs. When we worked in silos, we could be wasting time by duplicating each other's efforts or working on the wrong things.

As a leader of our team, I used vulnerability and humility to acknowledge that I didn't know everything. It was always my mission to ensure my teammates' perspectives were heard. I could've easily told them, "Let's just do it this way and go." Instead, I asked questions to gain their perspective which enabled me to learn alongside them. Then, I could delegate tasks downstream in the months or years to come, resulting in us scaling our business faster.

To avoid wasting time after a customer meeting, we would take 5–10 minutes to debrief and ask our team members the following:

- What problems exist?
- What problems can we solve?
- How will we solve them?
- Which role will each member of the team play?

Answering these questions as a team provided a level of clarity that allowed us to efficiently execute for the client. Not having these debriefs would be like having a football team running several different plays at once, each player thinking they're following the right play while the ball ends up nowhere near the goal line.

When I was a quarterback in college, understanding the clarity of the play the coach called was my number-one priority. I also had to articulate that play to my teammates in the huddle and make sure that we all understood. In an offensive huddle, there are 11 players that compete against the defense. Imagine if I called a play and three players thought we were doing one thing, while another player believed something different, and the remaining seven thought it was a third play altogether. Everyone would go in a different direction, and the quarterback holding the ball (yours truly) would be crushed by the defense. This happened to me once, and I promise it was as painful as it sounds.

Social Selling– Why Is It Important For Follow Up?

Social selling is another way to connect with a customer; however, these interactions are digital in nature versus in person contact. It leverages social networking sites, allowing sellers to target prospects and create relationships. The goal of social selling is to help sellers find new ways to close business deals and grow their customer base.

In today's digital age, salespeople have many sales tools at their fingertips to help them follow up with potential customers. Each customer interaction is unique, and each customer will have personal communication preferences. Throughout my selling journey, my curiosity inspired me to ask customers how and when they want to be contacted. My approach takes the guesswork out of how to reach them, increasing the odds they will respond to me. This is far more efficient and effective than using methods that customers can ignore. Sometimes we sellers can be our own worst enemy, making the job of selling way more complicated than it needs to be. We get caught up in the pressure of selling and fail to notice other simple ways to meet new people through different channels. Simply put, ensure you are using social media to learn about your customers and also engage with them.

For clients who use social media, one of today's most popular and easiest social tools for business is LinkedIn. Its search capability allows you to find people who work for companies you are targeting as potential customers. If your company has a budget to spend with LinkedIn, consider the Sales Navigator product, which allows personalized searches and connections. Steer clear of spamming customers with unsolicited connection requests without any substance or value. Yes, social channels make more information easily accessible, but don't forget to do your homework. Make each impression with a potential customer memorable in the right ways.

Businesspeople can use social media to stay in touch with potential or existing clients by sharing news or articles. Tagging a potential customer when you share a piece of news helps ensure that your target sees your post. I find that when I tag customers, they appreciate it that I thought of them when sharing relevant information. More importantly, I was able to show my customers that I listened and followed up.

Social Selling—Impacting Your Ability to Follow-up

According to the *ZoomInfo Blog*, these are the top 10 social selling tools on the market today:

1. LinkedIn Sales Navigator
2. Hootsuite
3. ZoomInfo ReachOut
4. LinkedIn Social Selling Index
5. Nimble
6. Reachable
7. Rfactr (Social Port)
8. Awario
9. IFTTT
10. Bambu[16]

Each one of these tools can help you win relationships. However, some tools can be overwhelming without proper training. Companies that put a value on training and clear internal messaging tend to have more success with tool adoption, and they establish a precise method for becoming successful. According to Propeller, "73 percent of salespeople using social selling as part of their sales process outperformed their sales peers and exceeded quota 23 percent more often."[17] Also,

"Sales reps who use social selling are 79 percent more likely to hit their sales goals than those who don't."[18]

Utilizing platforms like LinkedIn, Twitter, and even text messaging will help you increase your follow-up efficiencies. Data points from the *Zoominfo Blog* articulate this in detail below:

Texting

- Prospects who receive text messages convert at a 40 percent higher rate.

- However, sending text messages to a prospect before making phone contact decreased the likelihood of ever contacting that lead by 39 percent.

- Texting after contact leads to a 112.6 percent higher lead-to-engagement conversion.

Social Media

- Sales reps using social selling are 50 percent more likely to meet or exceed their sales quota.

- 96 percent of sales professionals use LinkedIn at least once a week and spend an average of 6 hours per week on LinkedIn.[19]

Try This Exercise

Take a minute to write down your thoughts on the following questions: Which of these statistics stand out the most? Of the different social media channels, which of these are you using daily? How do you believe your social selling compares to the statistics above? Are you surprised at your success rate with follow-up through social channels? Lastly, if you were to make a change to your social selling ability, which of these will you implement tomorrow?

Time for an honesty check. Are you finding as you read this book that you aren't always disciplined on following up and documenting key customer interactions? If so, that's OK. You are honest with yourself; very few people can admit their own skills gaps. Nice work! The next step is for you to adjust your mindset for documenting customer conversations, interactions, and follow-ups. Once this happens, you'll begin to see the value of following a disciplined process, and your customers will look at you differently—with *trust*.

As I grew in my career, I realized how much creativity and proactivity drive my core follow-up activities. I challenged myself to make follow up fun, and at times entertaining! I found that I had more success using my personality in my follow-up measures. It was easier to let my personality shine when I had prepared ahead of time, because I wasn't trying to think on my feet. A simple example is being curious by better understanding my customers on a personal and professional level. I wasn't afraid to ask customers personal (though not *too* personal!) questions. Connections are not always completely about the business. They're often also about certain topics which help you as a seller establish commonality and rapport. By learning personal things about your customers and then documenting those nuggets of information, you can ask questions about those topics in future interactions.

Don't get me wrong: There were days when choosing to do all of the follow-up activities became difficult. But so is choosing to eat healthily, joining a gym, or reading a book instead of binge-watching TV. I became so disciplined about documenting every sales call or meeting that I would not shut down my computer for the day until all of my documentation was complete. One of my former colleagues said, "Damn, Jacox, you're like a F&*^% robot!"

Contrary to how that might sound, it was a huge compliment describing my relentless behavior to document customer interactions. I also realized that I was able to set a positive example for other salespeople on my team. They saw the success I was having and would ask me questions about what I did differently. Most of the time when I chatted with another salesperson about it, I would find gaps in their ability to document in real time. When salespeople wait to document their notes from a conversation, they unfortunately, lose track of crucial information and don't always capture what was necessary. It's just how memory works, and if you don't take action against it you will always forget information.

Documentation is often the most-hated part of the job. Sellers just want to talk to customers and learn about their problems to find opportunities to offer solutions. But once you start documenting and using it to follow up, you'll see how these activities move relationships forward, keeping you one step ahead of your competition.

CHAPTER 5:

Ditch The Ego And Let Your Authentic Self Shine!

In Chapter 3, I shared some of the best advice I've received: "You can be right, or you can get what you want." When I first heard this advice, I didn't quite understand the lesson. I wanted to have both choices and wondered why I couldn't. I loved being right, and I loved getting what I wanted. I mean, who doesn't? As my experience grew, the problem became clearer: the solution was checking my ego.

During my career, I worked with a number of people who believed they were God's greatest gift to their customer. Usually when they were faced with adversity, such as losing an account or not being able to win the deal of a lifetime, they would blame others—even their customers!

Whether you're interacting with a potential customer or a colleague, the advice remains true, and I would advise you to think often about what is essential to you and what will help you win more relationships. That doesn't mean you have to be a doormat for people. There are times when it is essential to stand up for yourself. But when you find yourself arguing or disagreeing with others on ego or principle alone, then it's time to let go of wanting to be right and grasp getting what you want—a healthy relationship.

Ryan Holiday's, *Ego Is the Enemy,* is one of the great books on ego. Holiday does a marvelous job of articulating how success or growth in our careers can be dangerous, letting us forget our humble beginnings. When we feel that we have somehow made it or are a top expert in our field, we can quickly allow our ego to get in the way of taking your relationships to the next level. We quickly fall into the trap of being the hero not only of our own journey, but also of everyone else's. In the meantime, everyone around us can see that our ego has become our enemy. When emotions are high, it's easy to feel that we have all of the answers, but in reality, we never do—no one does.

> *"You can't learn if you think you already know. You will not find the answers if you're too conceited and self-assured to ask the questions. You cannot get better if you're convinced you are the best."*
>
> -Ryan Holiday, Ego Is The Enemy-

Your ego will always be the roadblock to learning and winning relationships, and until you check it, you will consistently find yourself in complicated relationship-based situations. Holiday writes, "Greatness comes from humble beginnings; it comes from grunt work. It means you're the least important person in the room—until you change that with results." But the ego is very good at hiding behind other thought processes. Let's take a look at how we can find it.

Signs Of An Ego Getting In The Way

Below are some warning signs that your ego might be getting in the way of helping you win more relationships:

- You talk more than you listen.
- You are afraid to ask questions and show weakness or lack of knowledge.
- Resentment comes easily to you. Remember, misery always loves company.
- You take credit for success rather than highlighting your team or others who helped you achieve success.
- Your point of view is the only one that matters.
- You don't have a daily gratitude practice.
- You spend time with people who always agree with you and never challenge your line of thinking.
- You always have to be right.
- You lack empathy for others and find it challenging to understand someone's hardship or circumstance.
- You don't like to roleplay or practice in your professional life.
- You rationalize your line of thinking to make you feel that your opinion is the only one that matters.

When our ego gets in the way, we put up walls that don't allow our authentic self to come out.

Try This Exercise

Write down some thoughts on what you think it means to possess an ego that gets in the way for someone. Can you think of a time when you may have been perceived as egotistical? What was the impetus that made you act that way? Were you trying to be "right" in that situation?

For some people, being their authentic self can be very challenging, especially in today's world. While some company cultures accept different races and creeds, others do not. It's not a perfect world, and many people still face civil rights and equality issues daily.

Recently, I attended an executive leadership conference that focused on diversity and inclusion. It was a profound few days! I learned so much and gained valuable perspectives. Our class of executives included different races, sexes, and sexual orientations. Early in the course, I had the opportunity to speak about racism in the workplace. When it was my turn to speak, I told the class that "I don't have a racist bone in my body, and I'm accepting of everyone." I truly meant what I said, but the leader of the class looked at me and said, "Why would you say that?" My defenses quickly kicked in. I felt attacked because I am genuinely accepting of others, but her point was, why did I *need* to say that. She pointed out that I seemed to be making myself feel better about any racist tendencies I might have without even knowing. I felt backed into a corner and embarrassed. She backed off, thankfully. Her point was not to embarrass me, but to make all of us in the class realize how delicate a conversation like this can be in today's social and corporate environments. As a middle-aged white male, I quickly learned how privileged my life is. It was a great lesson for me to always work on self-awareness.

For example, when I go to my car in a parking lot at night, I generally don't have to think about being mugged or violently attacked. Whereas, sometimes a female might have a completely different perspective or viewpoint based upon her potential fears that I might not even think about. If I visit an island where the entire population is white, I don't have the same worries or uncomfortable feelings as a black man would.

Too often I've heard people say they can't be themselves at work. I didn't understand before my diversity training, mainly because I was naive. I hope that as you read this, you seek consistency in your behavior and show your authentic self in conversations as much as you can. I realize that this advice might be hard to implement, since not every environment allows us to show our true selves. Do your best and try to make situations as positive and impactful for others as you can.

All of the strategies in this book can help you focus on being yourself. I am convinced that by practicing them daily, you can win more relationships. When you hide your real self, the listener may think they're seeing your ego rather than a mask you're wearing. Ryan Holiday says it best in this quote:

"When we remove ego, we're left with what is real. What replaces ego is humility, yes—but rock-hard humility and confidence. Whereas the ego is artificial, this type of confidence can hold weight. Ego is stolen. Confidence is earned. Ego is self-anointed; its swagger is artifice. One is girding yourself, the other gaslighting. It's the difference between potent and poisonous."

-Ryan Holiday-

I want you to think for a minute. Is there anyone in your personal or professional life who has the ego described above? Do you trust them with everything? With anything? Now think about people you believe in wholeheartedly. They're the same person in and out of work. That's why it's so critical to focus on being the best version of yourself you can be at all times. As we've discussed, trust is vital in winning the relationship. If you aren't authentic, people will find you less trustworthy, and you'll find yourself losing relationships rather than winning them.

Living Ego Free: The Value Of Being Vulnerable

As I mentioned earlier in this book, my willingness to be vulnerable enough to ask questions always helped immensely in my business career. There were many times when my team and I would meet with customers who would communicate their technical issues to us. Some of the technical words that I heard from customers sounded made up at times, but they weren't. When faced with the situation of not having a clue what they were talking about, my choice was to pretend I understood everything they were saying, or to ask them to explain. You might be thinking, "Weren't you scared of looking dumb or losing the customer's confidence in you?" No, I wasn't. Partly because my company's job was not to prove that we all had computer science degrees, but to help identify and acquire the right talent for them.

But another reason is my curiosity. It comes naturally to me, but you can learn to become curious about your customers, too. Some people will agonize over whether it's the right time to ask questions, but if you have a positive, curious tone in your voice, you will see positive outcomes by putting yourself out there to ask any question that you have. You should not be afraid to ask a question if it helps you learn and allows others to share their knowledge.

Many times throughout my career, my customers would thank me for asking questions. It became a personal goal to hear the customer say, "That was a great question, Casey!" Asking questions and not being afraid to say, "I don't know," showed my customers my authentic self. It showed them I was human. And it showed them that what you see is what you get.

Let me share an example when I was 14 years old and realized, even back then, my curiosity never prevented me from learning. It was my eighth-grade year, and I was selected to be a "Natural Helper." This was a group identified as individuals who possess good listening skills and could be there to help a classmate who might be going through a difficult time. One of our breakout meetings, we had a session on teen sex with my classmates. Now, what I heard the teacher say was something completely different. What I heard was "*team* sex." In my mind, I kept hearing the phrase "team sex" and tried my best not to laugh. I looked around and was speechless that everyone was so focused and wasn't giggling at least a little. My immaturity and pre-pubescent mind was truly getting the best of me and now I was committed to letting this scenario play out. Finally, I couldn't resist any longer and had to ask the question, in arguably, the most naked and vulnerable moment of my life.

I said, "Mr. Teacher, is team sex kind of like an orgy?"

Immediately, I felt 500 eyes staring directly at me. My classmates and the other teachers couldn't believe that I had asked such a thing.

My teacher replied, "Casey, what did you say?"

"You keep talking about 'team sex,' and I am really confused," I said.

Then laughter filled the gymnasium, and I was puzzled and embarrassed, but still wanted to learn.

My teacher somehow figured it out and told me, "Casey, I think you misunderstood. We are talking about '*teen* sex and **NOT** team sex.'"

Then, I laughed at myself. Bigtime. As did everyone else in the gymnasium.

Despite my embarrassment, I had pushed myself out of my comfort zone to ask a question since I was confused. I had several classmates come up to me afterward and tell me they were so impressed that I wasn't scared to ask such a question. That wasn't my goal, but it did win me relationships.

The same holds true when you are meeting with a customer. The customer might be sharing information about their business challenges or their product. If you don't know something or don't understand - ask them! They are the experts on their business and are willing to share information with you, only if you have the ability to ask. Where salespeople fail is by nodding their heads and making the customer feel like you truly understand what they are saying when that's not the case.

Try This Exercise

Write down what it means for you to be vulnerable and authentic. What words come to mind? Are there areas in your life where you can or cannot be your true self? Why do you think that is the case? Now the tough part: find a friend or a co-worker you trust. Ask them about when they've perceived you as being vulnerable and authentic.

How do your answers compare? I know this can be scary. But this is the key to getting to our vulnerable selves. We aren't perfect, and we never will be.

When I went through the exercise above, here's what came to my mind:

- Proper mindset: Do you find yourself complaining more than being grateful?

- Positive tone, written and verbal.

- Not afraid to ask questions, no matter how dumb they might be.

- Self-awareness: Do you ask for feedback often?
- Are you coachable?

- Positive self-talks: Conversations with yourself to create a positive mindset.

- Are you open to change or always resistant? If you are resistant to change, read Spencer Johnson's *Who Moved My Cheese?*

- Role-playing and the art of practice: Do you do whatever you can to avoid practicing in front of your peers, or do you enjoy the journey in learning?

Ego Wants Perfection: Be Open To Feedback

One of the most sought-after speakers, authors, and researchers is Brené Brown. Her TED Talk on vulnerability has been watched and downloaded over 40 million times! [20] Her book *The Gifts of Imperfection* directly teaches us to be imperfect. When you let go of trying to be someone you're not, you will open yourself up to newfound relationships that are out there waiting for you.

We all go through phases when our ego takes over, shining a negative light on us, creating hardship, and impacting relationships that you truly need to be successful. During these phases, our ability to win relationships is challenged by our inability to accept or even seek feedback.

Holiday says it eloquently:

"The art of taking feedback is such a crucial skill in life, particularly harsh and critical feedback. We not only need to take this harsh feedback, but actively solicit it, labor to seek out the negative precisely when our friends and family and brain are telling us that we're doing great. The ego avoids such feedback at all costs, however. Who wants to remind themselves to remedial training? It thinks it already knows how and who we are—that is, it thinks we are spectacular, perfect, genius, truly innovative. It dislikes reality and prefers its own assessment."

Feedback can be difficult to hear at times, but you'll be better prepared for it if you can start each day with these four thoughts:

- I'm not perfect.
- I will make mistakes and learn from them today.
- I will not always be the smartest in the room.
- It's OK to say, "I don't know."

I have kept these four thoughts in mind for the majority of my life. It wasn't always easy, requiring years of practice and an open mind. Good feedback should not crush your confidence, but keep you grounded and yearning for greatness. Whether it is your spouse, your best friend, your co-worker, or even your customer, challenge yourself to be open to how you are perceived and how you are acting. The benefits of accepting this mindset will help you immensely in winning relationships.

How To Move Forward—Ego-Free!

Often, leaders can create environments that allow employees to show true vulnerability. They aren't scared to make mistakes, but instead, are encouraged to take risks and learn from those mistakes. Such leaders generally use a Socratic method of leadership, which involves asking questions that will help the associates come to their own rescue rather than just telling them what to do. The Socratic method of leadership has been life-changing for me in how I deal with colleagues, customers, and friends when building relationships.

In researching the Socratic method, I learned from Thomas Metcalf, as he described how business leaders can use the Socratic method of asking students questions, so they find their own answers:

Since the questioning process is supposed to be collaborative, the leader needs to ask open-ended questions that allow team members to expand on ideas and listen carefully with no prejudgment. Socratic questioning is not interrogation; therefore, all need to be brought into the dialogue to generate a productive process. It is entirely appropriate to incorporate anecdotes, humor and props—whatever it takes to engage the team.[21]

Using the Socratic method worked wonders for me in my leadership experience. I had to challenge myself to try it at first, but once I did, the results were impactful; I saw my team grow and learn to think for themselves. Keep in mind that for the method to work, you need to foster collaborative environments where your team can take risks. It's worth the effort: it can produce amazing results and inspiring ideas because you've removed the ego from the equation.

Throughout my business career, I've seen many examples of how a leader's ego can cause countless people to adopt negative attitudes, which, in the end, breed a negative workplace culture. Unfortunately, these weak leaders make it too easy for their salespeople to take negative approaches in how they work with their teammates and, worse, with their customers. The more cynical the leader, the more transactional the sales environment—the short road to losing relationships and future transactions. Consultative, relationship-based salespeople need to put a stop to transactional sales environments. We need to lead by example.

The old saying "misery loves company" is all-too accurate. It's easy to talk about what isn't working or what someone said that was so out of line. If we ask ourselves the positive outcomes we get from having negative conversations, the list will be very short. Sometimes when a deal is lost, leaders talk about how the client doesn't understand what they're doing. Such negative talk in front of your employees breeds a culture of blaming others instead of finding ways to learn why you got outsold in the first place. As we've seen throughout this book, the power of vulnerability is central to selling. We need to determine what we could've done differently to win the relationship so we can win it next time. If we could sell without ever talking to a customer, by automating the entire process, salespeople would have been fired already. Social interaction builds connection and trust, both of which are necessary in today's selling environment. Selling is about being genuinely curious about another human being and actively listening to them. The feeling we get as humans when someone listens to us with intent to understand us is something technology will never replace.

On the other hand, when leaders create an environment where people feel comfortable saying "I'm not sure," or "I don't know," they foster a culture of honesty, learning, and growth. To me, part of the solution is when leaders are willing to be vulnerable with their associates. Associates and leaders alike can learn to be more vulnerable through mentorship. A large portion of my business career involved mentoring leaders and top sales performers. I loved this part of my job, since it gave me a daily opportunity to help others grow and find success. When I challenged them to learn new things, I sometimes found that I was asking questions that my mentee couldn't answer. I would quickly tell them that one of my favorite answers to any problem was "I don't know." By doing this, my mentee would become more comfortable in learning and less defensive when they didn't have an answer to one of my questions.

Sometimes my response would further confuse my mentee, which provided me an opportunity to use the Socratic method to teach. The power of asking questions to get others to think outside of the box and develop critical-thinking skills is one of the greatest gifts we can provide to any relationship we are cultivating.

I believe the power of vulnerability can be taught and adopted. To quote one of my mentors, John Kaplan, "It is OK not to know every answer—It is just not OK not to do anything about it." It's one of the critical things I shared with my mentees. Too often, salespeople will not admit what they don't know about a project, their pipeline, or even a new organization chart they are trying to penetrate. They try to bluff their way around the problem, with their body language and tone of voice giving them away every time.

Instead, they should be saying, "I'm not sure, but that is a great point you brought up. Let me look into it and get back to you." Or, "Mrs. Manager, I want to win this account and would love your support in helping me identify my gaps for where I might be missing information." By engaging in negative and, at times, toxic behavior, salespeople will often put up their defenses, which only prevents them from accepting the authentic learning.

My football coach at Central Washington, John Zamberlin, used to say frequently, "If you have to tell people how successful you are, then you aren't that successful." It was his way of helping us tame our egos. However, I've learned since then that in the right situation or environment, it is vital to show others what is possible. As leaders, it's OK to talk about what we are good at in the spirit of offering others the drive to accomplish more.

More importantly, at times, it's crucial to talk about where you've failed and what gets in the way of your success. It's about telling a story—positive or negative—to inspire teammates, employees, and even customers through real-life examples. Some of my most influential leaders or mentors have been insanely successful, and yet they had the knack of sharing their successes without using an arrogant tone.

Uncommon Relationships

I want to challenge you and others in your personal or professional life to be "uncommon" in the way you interact. Hall of Fame player and coach

Tony Dungy, who played in the NFL for four seasons and coached for 27 years—wrote a fantastic book on the topic called *Uncommon: Finding Your Path to Significance*. Dungy has faced plenty of adversity in his life, but with his uncommon way of thinking, he became the first black head coach to win a Super Bowl. Dungy has created great loyalty throughout his life by how he treats people. During his Hall of Fame speech, he said the most important part of his career was building relationships. Successful people are uncommon, and they are talented relationship-builders. Dungy's book reminds me of the opportunity we have every day to make uncommon decisions that will have a dramatic impact on our lives. These decisions can be around your diet, exercise, marriage, and relationships. It's common—and easy—to decide to eat fast-food and sleep in every day. The uncommon decision would be to eat a more balanced diet and get up three or four days each week to exercise. By making this conscience choice to be uncommon, you will begin to see results in a healthier body and mind.

Building relationships in our personal and professional lives can be simple, but also difficult and uncommon. It can be atypical in a marriage to help your spouse around the house. I've known many husbands and wives who have busy jobs and tell their spouse that "dishes aren't my responsibility." But helping out regardless builds a strong marriage and allows you more time with each other. Would you rather look for uncommon ways to help your spouse OR would you rather make your spouse feel that you are above those tasks and it's not your responsibility? Seems like a silly and useless way to live and a recipe for building unhealthy relationships.

Uncommon behaviors can prosper if we allow our vulnerability to shine through and use it to build stronger relationships.

Put Your Ego Aside: Be Open To Learning

In the staffing industry, high turnover is common amid salespeople. As someone who showed longevity in a volatile industry, I always challenged myself to show others the power of learning. Often, I would tell stories to newer associates to remind them that the Casey they see now is not the same Casey I was at the start of my career, in terms of day-to-day tasks and activities. I put in a lot of hard work to achieve success. To inspire a healthy and humble environment, I would often ask a newer associate to review a document or ask their advice about a scenario. The look on a new associate's face was priceless. They couldn't believe the top salesperson in the company was asking them for advice. Let me be clear: this act of vulnerability was not just for show. I would ask newer associates what they thought because I knew they had something to offer. I would give them opportunities to show me their critical-thinking skills and step up. I could see the culture changing for the better right in front of me. It was awesome!

My challenge to you is this: openly talk with your team and let them know that it's OK not to know everything. Remind your employees or teammates that we are always in a state of learning, and that should motivate us to grow and improve every day. Once we admit there is more to learn, we can get to the root of the problem or identify a creative solution much more quickly.

For example, when I was part of a team to lead a sales transformation (as described earlier in this book) within our company, we had hired external sales experts who taught us new and exciting ways to sell. They showed us how great questions drive positive outcomes for the business. In one of the most powerful moments of this training, a senior partner asked my group to answer a question we had proposed. Instead of guessing an appropriate answer, he asked what we thought. It blew me away that someone with that level of success would have the humility to ask us for the answer. Whether he realized it or not, he created an environment for learning, one that showed us we didn't have to always have the answers.

Cultivate Self-Awareness

An absence of self-awareness can lead to immense ego issues. When you lack self-awareness, you increase your chances of angering people, losing friends, and winning far fewer relationships. Someone who is not self-aware may come across as:

- Smug or off-putting
- Self-congratulatory
- Self-satisfied
- Cocky
- Not coachable

How can you become more self-aware?

While this skill comes naturally to some people, others have to work at it. One of the most impactful ways to improve self-awareness is keeping a daily journal. Write down your daily goals, plans, and priorities for the day, tracking which ones you completed. This exercise allows you to see what you've truly accomplished and what you might need to adjust.

A second way is to ask trusted friends or colleagues to describe you, having them share one or two things you're doing well and one or two things you need to improve.

Third, coaching can really heighten your self-awareness. Being coachable; however, is something everyone must realize at his or her own pace. You can either take constructive criticism or you can't. I learned this skill quickly through my days of playing quarterback in college, while at Central Washington University. When my quarterback coach was happy, it meant we had executed the play he called correctly. If my coach was unhappy about the outcome of the play he called, he made sure we watched it over and over – nearly 15 times! By providing this level of coaching, he showed us that in each play or each day of life, we always have opportunities to learn and get better.

If you're able to find ways to be coachable, I am confident you will add positivity to your life because learning can inspire people of all ages.

Your Online Social Ego

As sellers or business-development professionals, we are always seeking to impress our customers and win that relationship. The internet provides many online tools, applications, and social-media outlets to help us do that. We'll connect with customers through LinkedIn, Instagram, or Facebook, which can be a first step in taking the relationship further.

However, such a connection also contains a considerable risk if not taken seriously. As Joey Kolansinsky of Encore Electric told the Society of

Human Resource Management, "Social media has opened up the door for us to know people's intimate views on things that are not work-related."[22] This level of intimacy can allow us to be vulnerable with our customers, but it can also hurt us quickly. For example, pictures of you doing keg stands on Facebook most likely won't help you close the next big deal. Neither will engaging in a political argument on Facebook that everyone sees. Some of your customers don't care about your views on a particular ideology, but they might care how you treat others during an argument. Imagine that you're about to close a huge deal, having done everything you can to win it. You have become Facebook friends with your customer, and she reads some inappropriate and aggressive posts you made on Facebook. How will her views of you change? What if she cancels the deal based upon what she saw online? Would you be upset if your online behavior just impacted the outcome of a deal you've been chasing for months?

I'm not saying that you shouldn't be passionate about your views; but there is a time and a place for everything. When we allow ourselves opportunities to build genuine relationships, we create environments for having conversations on sensitive topics. By choosing to have these conversations verbally rather than on social media, we dramatically increase our chances of winning more relationships.

Use common sense and be aware of what you want your customers to see. A simple rule I recommend is never post anything you wouldn't want your mom, your teacher, your boss, or your child to see.

Many companies already have online social media policies, but these can be easily broken or misused. We might have a few cocktails one evening and share a harsh political view online that could distance us from our clients. While I think it's always better to remain professional online, the choice is still up to you. Be mindful of how your comments might impact your ability to win a relationship—and keep your job. According to a recent study by CareerBuilder, "A third (34 percent) of employers have found content online that caused them to reprimand or fire an employee."[23]

Choose your online photos wisely for your social business accounts. Customers don't need to see you riding a surfboard while sporting a Speedo in Hawaii, nor do they need to see you wearing your new leopard leotard. More appropriate, would be a photo of you wearing business casual clothes. Some people show pictures of their kids, which can work for some, but not for everyone. I love my kids more than anything, and I love to talk about them, but I've come to realize that not every customer feels this way about my kids. So why would I show pictures of them on my LinkedIn account?

Remember this – choose a photo that is safe and professional and presents you as a person that people would like to meet.

Ego Resists Change: Inspire Openness

It's essential to be open to change, not just for the sake of change itself, but also for the ability to understand other perspectives. Being open to change can offer new paradigms. In other words, being open to others' viewpoints or issues can help you better solve problems. Change is about more than just accepting others, however. It might be about changing habits that generate negative results, whether personal or professional. Change can be horrifying, but I am here to tell you, after watching others fail and then succeed, welcoming change can help you develop personally and professionally.

When I was on the sales transformation team, I saw how hard change could be and what an enormous payoff it could have on a company. The team was made up of top performers, either through sales production or sales leadership, which meant there was a lot of experience in the room, but there were also a lot of egos. As a team, our goal was to simplify our sales messaging to ensure that all of our salespeople could articulate the four problems that we solved for our customers. This would align our sales teams across the U.S. so our customers would enjoy a consistent customer experience.

My experience on this team provided an excellent test to be open to change and see what others had to say. It would've been easy to let my ego get the best of me and tell everyone else how I was right as the top salesperson in our company. Doing so would have been incredibly selfish: I might have felt good, but others would only feel stress and frustration. The team of people assembled in the room had multiple strengths and weaknesses. Some folks could articulate value well, while others struggled to think on their feet. Over the course of the week, we would break into groups to go through different sales-defining exercises so we could all agree on what problems we were solving, and then articulate our proof (customer case studies highlighting our success).

At times, I would be in a group where I was sure my ideas were right because I had "proof" (years of experience with customers) - me saying something or solving a problem for a customer. Yet, others might have their own proof based on their experiences.

Remembering Covey's advice to "seek to understand before being understood," I opened myself up to change. Before I spoke, I asked others their thoughts. Through patience and first trying to understand, I accepted that someone else's way might be as successful as—or more than—my own. We accomplished so much that week. We challenged each other often. Sometimes it was uncomfortable, and sometimes it was frustrating, but in the end, we simplified our sales message so we could now train more than 800 sales reps. What a great feeling!

One of my all-time favorite books, *Who Moved My Cheese?* by Spencer Johnson, is a fable that artfully shows why being open to change can offer positive outcomes. What I love most about this book is how it playfully uses mice to show how we humans get in our own way most of the time. Sometimes the most obvious answer is right in front of us, if only we can look at things more simplistically rather than through a lens of "my idea" or "what is 100% right." When people open their minds to change, growth moments happen. We become less afraid of change and more comfortable with hearing others' ideas. Too often in business, associates and leaders get so attached to their idea that they lose track of the big picture. In our personal relationships, a spouse, relative, or friend might be so focused on proving their point that they become spiteful—they don't want the other person to be right. We can choose to be confident in our view, but open to other views, as well. We might even learn something new. Positive outcomes not only impact us, but also our relationships. *Who Moved My Cheese?* teaches us that instead of seeing change as the end to "what we've always done," we should see it as an exciting beginning to what the future holds.

Personal and business relationships always ebb and flow. They require give and take if they are to withstand any problematic situation. When we restrict our openness to change, we limit our personal growth and reduce any chance to win a relationship. One of the characters from *Who Moved My Cheese?* says, "If you do not change, you can become extinct." Harsh, but true. Not being open to change or to different points of view, whether working with a new customer or discussing something with your spouse, can build a negativity inside of us that will continue to restrict our ability to build and win relationships.

The Art Of Practice Will Tame Your Ego

For those of you who played sports or an instrument growing up, I am sure you can recall a coach, teacher, or parent telling you this - *Practice makes perfect.*

"Perfect" rarely describes anyone or anything in life, but that doesn't mean we can't continue to strive toward perfection. When we don't seek opportunities to practice a skill in life, we are silently letting our ego prevent us from growing. One of the biggest mistakes we can make is not putting in 10,000 hours to become an expert at something, as stated by Malcolm Gladwell in his 2008 book titled, *"Outliers"*. Though the number of hours might seem daunting, in actuality, you can accomplish them in as few as five years, if you set aside time to own your craft.

    Whether you're a new employee or a seasoned veteran, you can never practice enough. Here's a story I loved sharing when I was training salespeople at a previous employer. The company logo contained the word "professional." While training, I would get the salespeople to agree that since we were professionals, we had something in common with professional baseball players. I would then ask them how often a Major League Baseball (MLB) team practices each week, both as individuals and as the whole team. Usually, my colleagues would guess seven days. "Actually, it's five or six days, depending on the team," I would reply. "Most MLB teams take Sundays off." Then I would ask how often we role-play different customer conversations so that we can drive value better. The typical answer would be once a week. How is it, then, I'd ask, that both salespeople and baseball players are professionals, yet MLB players practice five to six days a week, and we practice just once? How can we tell ourselves we are professionals, and then never practice? My team would quickly see that they needed to practice much more.

I loved my team's honesty. I was proud that my team admitted that they could do better. I would remind them that accepting our own gaps is half the battle. Salespeople are often reluctant to role-play, for fear of sounding stupid in front of their peers. The voice in their head says, "If I mess up, my buddies and my boss will think I'm an idiot, and I won't ever be able to change their opinion of me." Sound familiar?

Even more frightening, since they resist role playing, these same salespeople instead, are practicing on their customers! They respond to a customer complaint on the fly before practicing responses. When you think about how absurd this is, it is quite embarrassing.

Try This Exercise

Please stop and think for a minute. How often are you and your team practicing? Do you find excuses not to role play? If so, you might want to think about the impact of my example above. As you can see from my story, just a little practice could drastically impact the success for you and your team, collectively.

Let me share an example with you and take you back to the time where I wasn't fully prepared to become certified on our sales curriculum. It was my responsibility to know this content inside and out, and then be able to teach it to many other sales reps and sales leaders throughout our company. During our own training, we had to show our training vendor that we knew the content and could deliver the message with confidence. Remember, I had been with the company for nearly 20 years by this point and I was our top salesperson of all time. I knew my stuff, but I still needed to be coached.

Day one of training required us to present part one of the instructional information. Although I had practiced, I hadn't practiced as well as I thought. When it was my turn to present, I delivered the first round of content to our training vendor, our lead facilitator, and our CMO (Chief Marketing Officer). During my presentation, the body language I was receiving from the room was positive—I saw head nods, a lot of note-taking, and even a smile from time to time. When I had finished, our training lead asked how I thought it went. I told him, "I thought it went well. I am sure there were areas where I could improve, but the content flowed well."

He looked at me and then replied, "Casey, I am going to be honest. What I heard about you is that you are elite, and that was not an elite performance. Don't get me wrong, you did a good job, and I will pass you, but if you truly are elite, then I expect better from you."

I was stunned at first, and then became more and more angry. I wasn't mad at our lead facilitator; I was angry at myself.

Looking back on my performance, I realized I was not as prepared as I should've been. At the end of the day, our lead facilitator reminded us that we had one more day to deliver the next round of content. He said what a great day it had been, but he was excited to see who would take their game to the next level. As he spoke, I couldn't help but feel that his message was being delivered directly to me.

We concluded the meeting and made our way back to our hotel rooms. Some of my colleagues asked whether I could meet for a beer. I let them know that I had to work on a few things instead. I was still angry and couldn't wait for the next day so that I could redeem myself. I spent the next four hours delivering the content to myself in front of my hotel room mirror. I vowed that I would not let what happen today happen again tomorrow. I went over the material so many times that I almost memorized it. Finally, I decided I was ready. My practice and preparation were complete.

The next morning, I could feel my adrenaline building as soon as I got up. I was excited to present! We entered the room and broke into our smaller groups. My colleague wanted to go first, and I knew that I couldn't allow that to happen. I was so excited and anxious to go and told him, "Sorry brother, I'm up and I need to go first." Our lead facilitator said, "Alright, Day two ... let's begin the day, Casey."

I got up to speak, and when the first words came out of my mouth, I felt a sense of calmness and increased confidence, thanks to all the practice I had put in the night before. For the next 20 minutes, I delivered the content just like I had practiced. When I finished, our lead facilitator looked at me and said, "Great job. *That* is what elite looks like." What a relief that all my hard work paid off!

Practice is about committing the time daily, weekly, or monthly. Challenge yourself to limit the overall scope of your training so that you (or your team) don't get overwhelmed by the skills you're trying to sharpen. Remember that everyone is there to improve—even the leaders.

One effective way to rehearse is to pair sales reps with leaders and task them with calling each other, either on the way into work, or on the way home. The caller's job is to initiate a role-playing activity. Let's use fictional salespeople Bob and Susan as an example. Bob calls Susan and says, "Hi Susan, this is Bob from ABC Company, do you have a minute?" Susan jumps into role-playing mode and plays the role of the client. They do a five-minute roleplay where Bob tries to schedule a meeting with Susan. When I had my teams perform this exercise, not only did they get in more practice, but their ability and confidence to handle customer objections increased greatly.

Another method is a larger, team-interactive session. Each day, our company would have a 5–10 minute meeting to discuss the day's goals. During this meeting, leaders would also conduct a random role-play in front of the team. Then everyone else practiced. What I found in my experience was to have a leader go first. This would help calm the team and show them that he or she is just as willing to practice and find ways to improve as well. We quickly found that daily practice routines not only helped everyone get better, but they also strengthened the team relationships.

Salespeople Are Not The Only Ones Who Should Practice To Achieve Success

Each day, millions of people around the world board an aircraft to fly to a destination. Once we board the plane and buckle our seatbelts, we have zero control over what happens next. We put so much trust into airline pilots to find smooth air, avoid bad weather, and land the plane safely. Would you be willing to board an aircraft with a pilot who doesn't have the minimum amount of hours needed to be a pilot? Would you feel comfortable boarding a flight with a pilot who has never practiced? You might be thinking, this is crazy Casey, how can you compare a flight deck to a salesperson? Don't get me wrong, the risks of a pilot are far more extreme than most professions, especially a salesperson. However, I f you take a step back, there are some similarities which I will describe below.

Why do we expect our customers to jump into our "aircraft" when we aren't practicing our "flying" at all?"

Pilots go through thousands of hours of training before they can fly professionally, and twice a year, they must operate simulator flights with multiple emergencies if they want to keep flying. Cockpit Resource Management Training (later labeled as Crew Resource Management) has impacted the airline industry the most, mainly due to major aviation accidents in the 1970s. Cockpit Resource Management was implemented to enable pilots to check their egos and communicate more clearly. Additionally, this new process improved the relationships with other crew members on each flight.

In other words, airplane captains may say something is the "right" way, but they are still human and can make mistakes. Pilots initially thought Cockpit Resource Management would take away their decision-making authority in the cockpit. They didn't want things to turn into a democracy. That might make sense to some, but in the end, these pilots were resisting change.

Over the last 30 years, some of the most tragic air crashes have been caused by a lack of communication, or lack of camaraderie among the flight crew. Unfortunately, just like in the sales profession, it's been documented that some pilots have enormous egos and an inability to effectively build relationships with their co-pilots, flight attendants, and, most importantly, passengers. This type of toxic ego bred catastrophic results.

United Flight 173 on December 28, 1978, is one of the most well-documented cases of a crash resulting from faulty relationships, lack of self-awareness, and ego. The flight, piloted by an experienced cockpit crew, departed from Denver for Portland. Before departing, they had more than enough fuel, plus extra, to make the trip.

As the plane neared Portland International Airport and the crew initiated landing procedures, the plane vibrated abnormally and pitched at an unusual angle, even though the landing indicator light showed the gear had lowered successfully. They flew in a holding pattern for about an hour, trying to diagnose the problem—but no one was monitoring the fuel levels. During the approach into Portland, the number-one and number-two engines flamed out and the crew sent a Mayday. It was their last radio transmission. The plane crashed, 23 people were injured, and 10 died, including two crew members. After reviewing the crash, it became apparent that the flight deck lacked communication. The pilots didn't speak up and tell the captain the fuel was running low.

Another tragic airline disaster resulting from poor communication (a.k.a., improper cockpit resource management) happened to United Flight 727 while attempting to land in Salt Lake City. The weather was good during the approach; however, after being given instructions by air traffic control to descend at a certain rate, the crew did the exact opposite. Why? Because while the first officer was doing one thing, the captain was accidentally doing another, which increased the speed of descent beyond the plane's threshold. The FAA's official finding was that the captain had not taken "timely action to arrest an excessive descent rate on approach." [24] Again, if the crew had been better trained and pilots had been taught to improve their communication through relationship building, this accident would not have happened.

Just like pilots need to practice and communicate as a team, so must salespeople in order to be successful. How often do you resist change? How about others on your team? How often do you see your sales peers squirm at the thought of role-playing?

I remember hearing one salesperson say, "It is hard for me to practice real sales conversations, as I sound so different in front of the customer." I couldn't help but laugh at the naïve ego this person had when he said this. Unfortunately, he was wrong. Plain and simple, the more you practice, the better you will be at whatever you decide to do in life.

As you learned throughout this book, it's about reaching a positive outcome again and again. It's about building strong relationships with your team and your customers. It's about discovering and working on the gaps we all possess. By showing people you're open to change and that you value other perspectives and opinions, you immediately create environments where positive communication can occur. Lastly, you also realize that you won't always have all of the answers to solve most problems. When you can address these points listed above is when you will see positive environments established, where relationships are won together as teammates and leaders.

We covered a lot in this chapter. Ego is not always easy to overcome, mostly because of how it hides, but when we do overcome it, we become the people we are meant to be—the people we truly wanted to be all along. I would encourage you to review this chapter often for a self-awareness check. We all have egos, and we must constantly monitor how fragile they are, especially in unfavorable environments.

CHAPTER 6:

Success Takes Time —Be Patient And Persistent!

In today's fast-paced world, everyone wants immediate success. Some of us don't have the patience to realize that all good things must develop over time. Business leaders feel increasing pressure to grow their businesses faster. They are constantly challenged to innovate and meet the needs of the market, while keeping up with their competitors. At times, pressure to grow your business too fast can be unhealthy, and that pressure can filter down to salespeople trying to grow their accounts faster, faster, and faster. When some salespeople feel this unhealthy pressure, they end up turning sales relationships into unfortunate, transactional debacles. This is a prime example of why customers don't trust salespeople because they are always being pushed to "close the deal." Alternatively, if salespeople allow relationships to organically grow while they focus on solving problems and building trust, they will close more deals in the long run.

When businesspeople meet a potential customer or a key contact, they want to have success with that person immediately. Unfortunately, that is not how success works. If a customer is going to stand by you through the ups and downs, you will need to build a relationship first, and that takes time and patience. Both parties must persevere. You must rely on patience and resolve during times of uncertainty or business struggle. The seller must always resist any temptation to respond in anger to the customer or provoke them, as it will only alienate the customer. In negative, challenging environments, patience must shine through so that you increase your chance to win that relationship and avoid a negative outcome.

When you apply patience and persistence together, you increase your chance to succeed in every aspect of your life. Sticking to any plan takes patience, and one must understand there will be bumps along the way. If that plan or goal is really what you want, then you will gain the skill of perseverance to reach your desired outcome.

> **"Adopt the pace of nature;
> her secret is patience."**
>
> *-Ralph Waldo Emerson-*

Anything worth anything in life is not just given to us; it always must be earned. Emerson's advice above is timeless. Dating back to the early 1800s, character traits such as patience, love, perseverance, and generosity were being taught. Ironically, as a society, we are still struggling to adopt these very important life skills so that we can communicate more effectively in our personal and professional relationships.

Let me share a story about how I learned the power of patience. I still reference this lesson throughout my life today.

It was my football career that taught me how patience can positively impact your life. At 15, I was a skinny sophomore quarterback trying to find my way. My coaches used to joke with me and call me "steak and potatoes" to encourage me to eat more and put on muscle, since I resembled a large head on a toothpick. Given how violent the game of football can be, a football player needs to be strong to withstand the physicality of the game. I still joke that it was a miracle I didn't get broken in half during the tackles that would come my way.

At our high school, there was another quarterback my age that season, but because he was much more athletic and stronger than me, he was placed on the JV (junior varsity) team, while I was placed on the sophomore team. The JV team was made up of players the coaches thought would most likely be playing varsity shortly. It was where I wanted to be, but I didn't have the strength or athleticism yet to make it.

During that sophomore season, I played against kids stronger than me, and my team suffered through a lot of losses. We had some highlights, though, and managed to win a few games, which helped our confidence. Somehow, our undersized team stepped up to the challenge and showed our heart and grit and almost pulled out an amazing upset. Although we lost that game, we grew as a team. I grew as a quarterback and leader of that sophomore group. I remember taking some vicious hits and still getting up, hit after hit after hit. After playing a very talented team towards the end of the season, my sophomore team had a very memorable bus ride where relationships were strengthened, and I recall a great heart to heart conversation with coach Glen Dacus. He would share how proud of me he was, and I recall, some nearly 30 years later how impactful that was for me in maturing as a young man. My teammates and coaches began to see a toughness in me that I didn't even realize was there. On that bus ride back to our high school, our relationships as players and coaches grew. I was about to receive – I mean earn – a new opportunity.

Throughout that season, the coaches would tell me that my stock was rising because I persevered through tough situations and found ways to lead my teammates. Showing my naivete, I wondered, "What the hell does that mean, my stock is rising?" At 15, I wasn't dabbling in the market as a day trader yet.

With my improved play and confidence rising, I received an opportunity to play in the final JV game, splitting the time with the other quarterback. I managed to play well and lead the team to a few touchdown drives, which created a legitimate chance to compete for the starting quarterback position on the Varsity team next season.

After the game and leading into the offseason conditioning program, the other quarterback and I learned we would be competing for the starting quarterback position. This meant that I had the chance to be a two-year starting quarterback in high school! What?? How did this just happen?

I was shocked, but thrilled. The head coach, Marty Osborn, warned me that it would take a lot of hard work if I wanted this position. Coach Osborn and I set goals that would give me the best chance to win the starting quarterback position. I had months of hard work ahead of me. Coach and I would create a goal worksheet where I could track my progress on improvement. My goals consisted of strength goals involving bench press, squats, and power cleans, as well as speed goals, which included a 40-yard dash and a conditioning test before the fall season. The final conditioning test showed the coaches who had truly worked hard over the summer. Some 30 years later, I can still visualize the goal sheet pinned up next to my bed so I could always see it.

For the next five months, I arrived three days a week at 5:45 am for weight training. One of our offensive linemen made it his job to drive me to school those days and work out with me. I knew I was in for a new life experience when he showed up at my house in his old Toyota pickup with 1980 heavy metal blaring on the radio. All I remember was him saying, "Get in, let's go lift and get strong."

When I entered the weight room, Coach Dacus was already there and I remember vividly him pointing to two different signs that were hung. The first one said, "Lift or Leave" and the second read, "No hats in the weight room." I still chuckle as I think back to those days, yet I'm so thankful for those opportunities. Looking back, that is when my life began to change.

After school, I had more weight training. On alternate days, I would stay after to throw the football to receivers who would run routes for me. I would throw the football with anyone I could find. I wanted this job badly and was willing to commit everything into the process.

Anything worthwhile that you want in life, whether it's a job, a promotion, or a relationship will take time, patience, and perseverance.

Here was my first real test and lesson in life, and I was ready for the task. All during spring football, the quarterback competition remained tight. Throughout the summer, I continued with the same running, lifting, and throwing regimen to give myself every opportunity to win this position. In August we reported to football camp, and the competition only heated up. One day I was on fire, and the next, my classmate was. After a see-saw battle right before our first game of the season, Coach Osborn came up to me while I was stretching with my teammates and asked, "Are you ready to be our starting quarterback?" My heart started racing, and I said, "Yes, Coach!" He said, "The job is yours, and you won it. Now go lead us to a winning season."

I barely restrained myself from jumping up and down like a six-year-old who just got the remote-control car he always wanted for his birthday. I put in so much time, effort, and hard work to achieve my goal, but I finally did it. On my drive home from practice, I couldn't wait to tell my parents the good news. I almost had tears in my eyes. So many times,

I had wanted to quit; the odds had been stacked against me. But I didn't. I chose to lift weights when I didn't want to. I chose to push myself and my teammates to run passing routes, even on days when the weather wouldn't cooperate. The patience required along the way would test my will, but I never gave up, and once I passed the finish line, I knew the journey was worthwhile.

As hard as this experience was, it prepared me for the challenges of being a salesperson. The time it takes to earn a new customer or meet a new sales target, takes time and clear goals. Little did I know that goal-setting habit would later help me achieve greatness in the business world, too!

Patience And Persistence In The Workplace

Relationships in the workplace are the foundation that moves the business forward. They drive products to market and win new customers. In the most simplistic terms, salespeople must build commonality and rapport with their colleagues and their customers to establish trust.

Think about when a new employee starts. We've all been the low person on the totem pole at one point. We didn't have all the answers, and we had our fair share of anxiety as we tried to impress our peers and leaders. I am very fortunate that great mentors and leaders taught patience and guided me to remain confident while learning and gaining experience. I took pride in making sure I offered that same level of tolerance and support to my own new employees. I wanted to treat them as I had been treated (remember Chapter 1?). Losing patience and freaking out only creates more problems, while remaining calm and focusing on patience helps new employees ramp up because they gain confidence more quickly.

> *"To be kind is more important than to be right. Many times what people need is not a brilliant mind that speaks but a special heart that listens."*
>
> -Unknown Author[25]-

While many skills are critical to patience in the workplace, as Chapter 3 showed us, the art of listening is especially important. When your employees or customers realize that you are actively listening, your relationships will become stronger and patience will come naturally. When you can show patience in tense moments, you will make your colleague or customer feel heard and nurtured. As I look back on my experiences, I can say that those were the defining moments of some of my most significant relationships.

Perseverance is just as essential in business, especially for salespeople. When you start a new sales job, you have to learn new skills, but you must also learn how to persevere with your customers. You have to get used to hearing the word "no" over and over again. Cultivating perseverance requires laser-like clarity on what you are selling and where you are going. You must truly understand the core problem your product or service solves for your customer. You must understand the goals you are setting each day, week, month, and year. Without that clarity, you won't be able to persevere through anything because you won't know why you are doing it.

One of the most reliable ways to master perseverance is with a positive attitude. This might sound simple, but it requires focus, commitment, and resolve. Albert Einstein once said, "Weakness of attitude becomes weakness of character."[26]

It took Einstein years of hard work, studying, and constant research to make the scientific and mathematical advancements he did. While we don't have any definitive proof, it's impossible to imagine that he would have made such achievements if he hadn't kept a positive attitude. You need to maintain a mindset that nothing worthwhile comes easy. The best salespeople I ever worked with had this mindset and persevered; they showed people that they could roll with the punches, gaining the respect of others and builder stronger relationships.

On *The Peak Blog,* Susan Halliwell writes, "A good salesperson sees the forest through the trees and success despite immediate odds. Great salespeople run marathons rather [than] face short challenges."[27] I love this quote. I have never met a sales or business-minded person that only saw success in their career. Everyone who has succeeded has learned through their failures.

"Failure is simply the opportunity to begin again, this time more intelligently."

-Henry Ford-

Failure teaches us that we must dig in and apply perseverance and patience to continue the race. We constantly must remind ourselves of that end goal or outcome we are seeking. As I mentioned earlier in this book, Stephen Covey teaches us to begin with the end in mind. That principle will help you always remember why you are doing what you are doing.

I learned a lot about perseverance during my career. As a salesperson, I was measured by revenue, profit, and the number of consultants I hired for my customers. Early on, there were months where things couldn't go wrong and the job seemed so easy, but then the next month, everything seemed to go wrong and the job seemed impossible.

One day, I vividly remember the feeling of losing half my business overnight. While I felt sorry for myself, I knew that sulking wasn't going to change my outcome. I knew that to change my outcome, I had to get back on the phone and go out and meet new customers. I had to keep prospecting and keep the sales funnel or pipeline full of potential opportunities for me to go and win new relationships. This is why it is so important to surround yourself with positive teammates and leaders who can pick you up when things get fierce in business. It's not a matter of *if* things get tough, but *when*.

Sharing and talking about your goals often with your leader or team is crucial. There were times when my team or leader would pick me up emotionally when I was having a tough day and remind me of the goals that I set for myself. They would ask me if what I was doing today would help me reach those goals. They weren't questioning me in a condescending way, but rather in a positive, motivating way. I had to be open to hearing their feedback; more importantly, I had to be open to receive their encouragement and not be defensive. I had to show my vulnerable side and be willing to ask for help, or show what I didn't know. When all of those conversations or thoughts came together, I truly grew as a person. If you're open to learning from these and others' experiences, I am convinced that it can happen for you as well—but only if you allow others to pick you up when you might not even think you need it.

What Does This All Mean?

When you have patience and perseverance, you have what Angela Duckworth calls *Grit*. Her book is one of the best books I've read on the subject. In it, Duckworth investigates why some people succeed while others fail, and she concludes that grit is the key.

In her TED Talk, she explains that "to get good at anything requires sustained interest and commitment, plus incremental improvement and the capacity to weather failure and setbacks."[28] Duckworth explains that to be great or to achieve excellence requires passion. That passion, deep inside of us, generates laser-like clarity on what we want to do and helps us persevere through tough times.

The South African College of Applied Psychology (SACAP) shares five common characteristics for someone they define as having grit:[29]

- Courage
- Conscientiousness
- Perseverance
- Resilience
- Passion

We've already discussed perseverance and patience. How can courage, conscientiousness, and resilience in the workplace help you become an elite seller?

As I think about courage, conscientiousness, and resilience in the workplace, I immediately think of all the tough days in my journey. When we see someone at the pinnacle of their career, we easily see their success, but not the difficulties of getting there. More importantly, we don't always see the challenges of staying on top.

Courage is often used to describe physical bravery, such as being a soldier on a battlefield. Yet many people show courage each day in the workplace. They stand up for themselves when no one else understands them or their perspective. As a salesperson, I had to continually show courage to my team when we would go through a business down cycle. Naturally, people reacted with negativity, often wanting to give up. The courageous person decides to march on, showing up to work the next day and working to build new relationships that will help pick business back up. Let's face it, in such a competitive world no one is going to take time to feel sorry for us, so we must learn to have the courage to achieve our goals.

Conscientiousness can also help you get to the top. It has helped me win many, many relationships—internally and externally. SACAP defines conscientiousness as "the personality trait of being thorough, careful, or vigilant." And it makes sense. *Thorough* relates to grit and staying on task to finish a job. *Careful* is about striving to be mistake-free and choosing words wisely when working with associates and customers. Lastly, *vigilant* reminds us to never give up, even when the cards are stacked against us. It's always easy to give up, but you must remind yourself that *someone* is going to be successful. *Someone* is going to win that account. *Someone* is going to build a relationship with that COO or CMO. Why can't that someone be you?

Resiliency is a character trait I've shared throughout this book. I've talked about my personal failures and successes and shared the resilient ways others achieved their goals. Let's face it, you are going to have ups and downs in your daily job. You are going to work with people you don't like or don't respect. You might even get fired or see that person you don't like get promoted, even if you don't think they deserve it. *Who cares?* Stop wasting your time on those thoughts. We can't control those things, but what we can control is our attitude and how we handle those tough situations.

According to Heads Up mental health organization, "Resilience is more than coping, however. Resilient people are also flexible, adapt to new and different situations, learn from experience, and are optimistic and ask for help when they need it."[30]

If you can apply grit—courage, conscientiousness, patience, perseverance, resilience, and passion—to your goals, if you can keep your eye on that goal, and if you can realize that each day will be a new test, you will be on the path to winning more relationships.

CHAPTER 7:

Win The Relationship – Personal Life Examples Beyond Selling.

The art of winning the relationship has many more possibilities outside of the business world. As the years went by, I realized how I could apply this philosophy to other facets of my life. The core mantra—"Win the Relationship, Not the Deal"—is a choice that usually targets aspects of our ego. At times, this mantra is annoying and difficult to say, much less practice, and those are the days when I need it the most.

When we find ourselves frustrated or irritated by something, we should stop and ask why, correct? Is it worth the anger we're generating? If we are honest with ourselves, this should be an easy answer – it is not.

Researching and writing this book was one of the most fulfilling journeys of my life because it forced me to think about so many different examples that I could share with you. Below, I will take you through a few examples of how my mantra can help us all win relationships in our personal lives.

Win The Relationship, Not The Dementia

Over the last 15 years, I've been helping manage my father's declining health, which is now a rap sheet of medical conditions, including dementia. Dementia is an awful disease that disguises who your loved one is and, at times, makes you forget who they once were. The journey of taking care of my father both financially and emotionally has been extremely taxing, and I couldn't have supported him without my wife, who has been an absolute rock!

Just like with your customers, if you try to convince someone with dementia to do something, or that you are right and they're wrong, they will always resist you. However, when we meet them where they are, listening to them and asking questions of value to them, we win not just the transaction at that moment in time, but also the relationship with our loved one.

At first, I didn't understand how to have a long-term relationship with my father and his dementia. I've learned that I must play the role of a thespian and be able to quickly act on my feet. As do comedians on an improv stage, I was tasked with the same challenge numerous times during visits with my father.

On one visit, I entered his bedroom to find him asleep as usual. It took me roughly 15 minutes to wake him up out of a tired state and for him to realize who was there to see him. He smiled and thanked me for coming. He asked how my wife and the kids were. The conversation continued in a positive direction for a few minutes before it took an abrupt negative turn.

Out of the blue, my father looked at me sternly and asked, "Where is all of my money?" Confused, I replied, "What do you mean, Dad?"

He became agitated and then asked me, "Why did you steal all of my mother-fucking money to build your house?"

OUCH! That stung.

I immediately went into defense mode and couldn't believe he could say such a thing. I wanted to tell him how if we hadn't stepped in to help all of those years, he would have been dead or living in a van down by the river by now.

I knew the visit was over and was thankful that my kids and wife had not been there to experience it. I told my dad that I loved him and said that I would see him soon. I had to remove myself from the conversation and get out before it got worse. Once a person is lost in a moment of dementia, you can't reason with them. To this day, my father has no recollection of saying such a thing, nor will I bring it up to him. I had to lose this "transaction" and give up being right to get what I wanted: my father being calm and happy.

Winning the relationship with my father is about the long term. It has challenged me not to "win" the visit, the transactional moment, just as we salespeople have to think about when meeting with a customer. I've used all the points of winning the relationship: I practice the Golden Rule by treating him with the respect I would want someone to give me. Setting proper expectations for myself over what a visit might look like helps me maintain a positive mindset. Additionally, I often found that journaling my thoughts or taking a moment to talk about my thoughts or feelings out loud helps me stay present during a visit. I listen to my dad and his reality at that moment. I ditch my ego and the need to be right so I can be authentic with him. Most importantly, I practice patience.

Since I've been working hard toward this goal, not all our visits have been negative. The one constant story my father brings up is how proud he is of his grades. In those moments, he truly believes he has just finished another quarter at the University of Washington or Central Washington University. The first time we heard about this fantastic scholarly achievement, my kids and I were so confused. Quickly, I realized what was happening—the dementia was back. Instead of arguing or reminding him that he graduated 50 years ago, I said, "Dad, that's awesome! Congratulations! Tell me, what do you think you did this quarter versus last quarter to improve so much?" The assisted living facility even created a certificate congratulating my dad on his grades since this is a repeated state of mind for him that doesn't go away. Playing along with what he believes to be true is now the only way to ensure we have positive visits.

    Throughout this journey as we've talked to medical professionals, this is exactly how we are supposed to deal with a loved one that has this awful disease. At first, I felt like I was patronizing him, but it is not in actuality. I became a character in my father's new reality and it is the only way to find peace. Arguing with him would only upset him and make him cling harder to his reality. Being with him in his reality helps my father stay calm. One thing for sure is that going into actor mode makes us smile more as a family and enjoy the visits.

Win The Athlete, Not The Game

In today's fast-paced world, nothing seems to be more out of control than youth sports. Not only are kids being asked to work harder, invest long hours in training, and commit to one sport exceptionally early in their lives, but parents also think it is OK to scream profanities at referees and obsess over the outcome of the game so much that fights sometimes do break out. Coaching youth sports is challenging at the best of times, but it's even worse when the child is only there at a parent's command.

Coaching youth sports is about more than coaching a child to be a better player. It's about building confidence, self-motivation, goal-setting, and overall team attitude. It's about finding that unique characteristic inside a person and providing a small spark to help ignite a fire that produces exciting results for another person. I was able to do that by winning the relationship with one young baseball player in particular.

Jared (not his real name) was an older player on our team and one who was not as athletically talented. He lacked motivation from the start of the season, and at times I questioned why his parents signed him up for baseball at all. His lack of interest in the game made him very difficult to coach, but my assistant coach and I refused to give in. "What an opportunity!" we thought to ourselves.

We often talked about ways to make the game fun for him. What drills could we do to keep him engaged? What questions could we ask? How could we praise him and build his confidence when he would always strike out? As coaches, we always challenged our players to stay in the game mentally. We encouraged talking about the game and the situation so that everyone would know what to do with the ball when the ball was hit to them.

Jared decided to take this to the next level and surprised us with his creativity. Instead of yelling the traditional short words of encouragement, like "two out guys, the play is at second," Jared would yell streams of advice, like, "Here we go, RBI time! Runner at first, a runner at second! Let's throw it and get him out!" It would bring a smile to our faces knowing that we were starting to break through with him.

Sometimes his patter would contradict itself and confuse us, but we decided to praise him for finding his purpose. During the season, we named a player of the game after each game. Usually, this was someone who performed the best: the best pitcher of the game, the infielder who made a diving play at shortstop, or the batter who successfully hit the ball.

One game, we named Jared the player of the game for showing his leadership by staying in the game every pitch and telling his teammates what to do if the ball was hit.

I can still see the look on his face: surprised eyes and a smile because he had won something and was being celebrated in front of his teammates.

Later, I received the following text from his parents:

Casey,

We are just so proud of what you have done with him. You have had a significant impact on his life and in so many ways! If you only knew Jared before, he really lacked confidence and just wasn't happy. Not to mention a lot of focus issues. Just playing for you has changed so much in that! You have made a mark in his life none of us will ever forget.

Instead of trying to win transactions with Jared— trying to get him to participate in the game the way the other players did—my assistant coach and I focused on finding ways to develop Jared for the long term. Keeping kids focused on their long-term development rather than the short-term outcome of a game or a season can make or break a kid's confidence.

Many of these challenges can also manifest when you are trying to coach a team of salespeople who are also only there because they have to be, or who are also only looking at the short term. Unlocking their self-motivation is as simple as taking the time to help them create success.

Covey writes in *Seven Habits*, "Begin with the end in mind." I always focused on the outcome I wanted for each child when I coached, and I can apply the same ideas to coaching my team. There is no possible way that I would have 12 all-stars, but I can have a realistic goal of developing 12 great human beings. When I focus on building character rather building egos with stats, I know I am helping them in the long run in the wild game of life.

Win The Marriage, Not The Boat Launch

Let me share one more way to use this philosophy, this time with a more lighthearted and comical anecdote. If you have ever navigated a boat launch, you know that it can be a stressful life lesson in winning the relationship (your marriage) rather than the transaction (launching or bringing in your boat).

My family and I had the luxury of witnessing a gem of seamanship from the small harbor near the boat launch. My red flags went up when I saw him driving his truck around the corner and then backing down the boat launch at high speed. Somehow, he managed not to jackknife the trailer, got it straight into the water, and secured the boat to the trailer.

At this point, his wife politely said, "Honey, did you pull the prop up?"

He dismissively said, "Of course."

He got back into the truck and had nearly peeled out of the boat launch when the sparks began to fly. The amount of shrapnel dragging on the ground quickly caught everyone's attention, except for the confident husband hauling the boat. The noise alone should have alerted the husband that something wasn't right. Not only did he miss the sound, but he also ignored the many eyes staring at the uncomfortable scene he was creating.

Common sense might tell you to stop the truck at the first loud screech, but instead, the husband must have wanted to show everyone how durable his prop was, so he dragged it a good 10 feet more.

Finally, he stopped and got out of the truck. His wife, understandably angry because she asked him about the prop earlier, said, "I thought you said you pulled the prop up!"

Angrily, he said, "I did, but I guess not high enough."

The husband was now mad at his wife for questioning his boating skills, so instead of owning his mistakes, he told her he had everything under control.

She asked him again, "Are you sure you have the prop high enough?"

He looked at her like she was the biggest idiot and said, "Are you serious?" It was amazing how strong his confidence was as he walked back to the truck. He again started driving up the boat launch but, unfortunately, he still did not have the prop high enough, so he took those blades for another spin down concrete lane. This time, he dragged his prop for a good 20 feet before stopping and finally getting the propeller high enough.

If this boater had ditched his ego and hadn't been afraid to ask for help or look for other solutions, he could have prevented his embarrassment—and the damage to his boat. More importantly, he could have avoided insulting his wife's intelligence and making a complete ass of himself while everyone was watching. I can only imagine the argument that ensued when they got home. Awkward! Clearly this boater let his ego get the best of him and chose to win the boat launch, not the marriage.

The story of the angry boater hits home for me as I've had to choose the exact opposite approach in my boating career given my lack of boating skills. Yes, I admit it. Thankfully, I've learned the art of self-awareness and have embraced the ability to make fun of myself, often. Don't get me wrong, I am not that bad, at least in my mind. I still have the ability to pull a water-skier or take an afternoon cruise without injuring anyone. Where I struggle is backing down the boat trailer when the boat launch is crowded – more than one small watercraft.

As I type this, I can feel the anxiety building. I start to hear the voices in my head. Turn left. Wait, no right. No Left. Shit! Then I hear my wife yelling, "Stop! You're about to hit the dock." I wasn't that close, again, in my mind. Unfortunately, my kids and even the dogs sided with my wife as key witnesses in solving this case.

This moment I've described is how I've learned (still not perfect) to embrace my gaps, slow down and ask for help. I'm not saying that I've quit my goal of getting better at this skill, but I've instead decided to focus on accepting where I can get better. Easily, I could let my ego get in the way and yell at my wife, but in the end, what does this solve? I only frustrate myself and create negative energy inside my family. And I would rather crash my boat down the dock, thoroughly embarrass myself, and lose a ton money due to my ego. I've utilized the same things I've written about throughout this book to Win the Marriage and not the boat launch!

All of these personal stories show that we have a choice in every interaction whether to win the relationship or hurt our ability to form healthy relationships. These stories may or may not make you the best child, coach, or boater, but by asking for a little help and being aware of your actions, you can improve your relationship with your parents, players, teammates customers and spouse.

CHAPTER 8:

Finish Strong!

Putting It All Together: Winning Your Relationships

You picked this book up because you wanted to win more relationships. I hope now that you are near the end of this reading journey that you have newfound clarity on what you need to do differently. That you are ready to take steps to try implementing these small, simple life strategies to succeed.

We all sail off course sometimes. We don't do this on purpose; it just happens. We can quickly get so set in our ways that we genuinely believe we are always right. But remember what we learned in Chapter 5 (ditch the ego) - Thinking that our way is the only way sabotages the relationships we are striving to forge. Can you recall a time as a seller where you were so excited to say what you wanted to say that you failed to listen to your customer? I know I can, and as I look back, it is not a good feeling.

As you recall from Chapter 3, God gave us two ears and one mouth, so let your ears do more work. The best sellers I've ever worked with were able to ask thought-provoking, open-ended questions that allowed the customer to talk and talk and talk. When customers are talking, you are learning about them personally and about their business.

And while they talk, put Chapter 4 into action by documenting what you hear and reviewing it with them.

Let your customers know when you will be following up, putting Chapter 2 (setting proper expectations) into action. This strategy also allows us to establish trust, because when we follow up when we say we will, the customer knows that you were paying attention and followed up as instructed.

Most importantly though, Chapter 6 teaches us to be patient and let your relationships happen organically. Time is your best asset because it allows relationships to grow.

Nothing sustainable is built in a day, a week, a month, or even a year. In *Outliers*, Malcolm Gladwell talks about his 10,000-hour rule. To become an expert at something, he says, you need to invest 10,000 hours. If you spent 20 hours a week working on being the best salesperson you can be, you'd become an expert in 10 years. Can you do that? What happens if you put in more time each week? Could you condense the time to 8 years, or even 5? Do you think you could stay that focused? You are the only one who can answer that question for yourself. For me, I answered yes to all of them and I exceeded what I thought success truly looked like.

Another word for *expert* is *elite*. When I think of elite people, I think "best of the best." I think of the people at the top of their field who always seek improvement. They are the leaders in their offices, locker rooms, bands, teams, classrooms and associations—any place they put their effort.

More often than not in my experience, I see companies consistently pressuring salespeople to win more deals and maybe gain a few relationships. This approach is the cause of the high turnover rate in the sales industry. It's not just the areas you would expect, such as car sales or retail. You see turnover in copier sales, real estate, the staffing industry, software sales, you name it.

We can agree that selling isn't easy, but the method I've developed throughout my career turns the impossible into the possible. Sales careers have plenty of ups and downs that can challenge your mental fortitude. I know; I've worked in sales for 20 years.

There were days when a customer misinterpreted something I said, causing friction in a relationship I was striving to cultivate. Chapter 1 teaches us to treat people the way we wanted to be treated—the Golden Rule. That's why we need to own our mistakes instead of pretending they didn't happen.

Remember: Chapter 6 teaches us that relationships take time and perseverance. Grit will get you through tough times, too. By following these strategies, you will reach the end of the rainbow. While you might not always find a pot of gold, a stable relationship can lead to more robust relationships, which could lead to a new business deal. We somehow find ways to make relationships messy and difficult when they don't need to be. When you choose the transactional path, you'll experience adverse outcomes, such as lost accounts and negative gossip about you from inside your own company. When you choose the consultative, customer-centric path, your confidence will increase, and you will build new relationships and strengthen existing relationships.

If selling were so easy, everyone would do it. The pressures to grow your book-of-business year after year can cause burnout, which leads to voluntary or involuntary turnover. Some salespeople leave just because they believe they will have more success elsewhere. If they're not working on building relationships, they'll have a tough time making that belief come true. I don't care who you are or where you work, if you choose *not* to follow these six simple strategies for building solid, foundational relationships, you *will* eventually lose. I've seen it happen again and again.

I didn't create the strategies I've shared with you; I've picked each one up along the way and blended them into my life. Life is complicated, and relationships are hard work, but if we simplify our actions, we invite better emotional outcomes and win more relationships. I know with all my heart that after 43 years on this beautiful earth and 20 years of relationship-based selling, the strategies I've laid out in this book will help you stay on course. When you practice these strategies daily, you will find more happiness in your life, and more of your relationships will flourish in both your personal and professional lives.

My last exercise is more of a task. Take a picture of the strategies and chapters below.

- **Chapter 1:** Follow The Golden Rule. Always.

- **Chapter 2**: Always Set Proper Expectations.

- **Chapter 3**: Don't Just Hear Your Customers, Listen To Them.

- **Chapter 4**: Always Document And Follow Up.

- **Chapter 5**: Ditch The Ego And Let Your Authentic Self Shine!

- **Chapter 6**: Success Takes Time – Be Patient And Persistent.

Then post them near your computer where they will always remind you how to consistently win more relationships. Snap a picture of the strategies in your office and post it to your social media, tagging me (@caseyjacox9 on Instagram, @CaseyJacox on LinkedIn, @CaseyJacox on Twitter, or @winningtherelationship on Twitter.) Together, we can build a community of sellers who are committed to building more relationships.

Thank you for investing in yourself and for taking the time to read to the end. I hope that I've helped you look at your own life differently as you begin to build stronger, more impactful relationships.

Author Casey Jacox

Author "WIN the RELATIONSHIP, not the DEAL"
The Quarterback Dad Cast – Podcast
Founder - Winning The Relationship, LLC

With more than 20 years of business experience, Casey's leadership helps companies emphasize the building of relationships and not just transactional business deals. For nearly half of his career, he was his firm's all-time leading salesperson. He's a father, a husband, a coach, a friend, a speaker and a business leader who brings his authentic self to work.

Over his entire career, adversity has always made him stronger. Casey is blessed to have a positive attitude, as he always looks at life through the eyes of an optimist. He loves to meet new people and has an intense passion for building relationships – true relationships that are long-lasting. He loves to laugh and make those around him laugh; if we are not having fun, then why do we go to work? He loves to empower people to achieve more than they think they are capable of. Competition is something he thrives on and is always pushing himself and others to compete so that clients will win by receiving his team's best effort.

Casey loves changing customer perception, and thoroughly enjoys opportunities to educate customers – showing them how they can achieve their business goals.

Additionally, giving back is a huge part of Casey's life. You have to pay it forward so that you are open to receiving in the future. Every day we are judged by who we are or what we do. As a former collegiate quarterback, Casey coach's youth sports alongside his daughter and son. He is the President of Tahoma Basketball Association which serves the Maple Valley community (over 200 athletes and 20 teams for boys and girls). Casey also sits on the Central Washington University Foundation Board which works with the University to plan and fundraise for large capital projects. Previously, he was an Executive Board member of Gloria's Angels and The First Tee of Greater Seattle.

He loves to read, do old man CrossFit, play golf, travel, embarrass his kids, and most importantly spend time with his family.

You can follow Casey's podcast titled "The Quarterback DadCast" which can be found in all of the major podcast outlets.

If you'd like to connect with him, please email him at:

ACKNOWLEDGMENTS

To my wife Carrie, it's been an amazing journey of growth starting all the way back to 7th grade and I love you with all of my heart. You are always a step ahead of me and I can't begin to tell you how much you mean to me. Your final efforts in helping me finish this book were so instrumental and this project would never have been completed without you! Thank you for your support, always!

To my parents, Mike and Judy Jacox (Killian) for teaching me the value of hard work and always instilling humility inside of me.

To all of my teachers and coaches who held me accountable and pushed me to be my best. You believed in me and provided me confidence to grow and utilize my god given potential. Specifically, Marty Osborn, Glen Dacus, Eric Anderson, Ed Gutierrez, Matt Sirotzki, Charlie Kinnune, and Jeff Shumake.

To all of my college coaches who taught me so much about handling adversity, goal setting, and being coachable. Specifically, Beau Baldwin, John Picha, Bruce Walker, Jeff Zenisek, Charles Chandler, Keith Ross, Brian Strandley, Ryan Fournier, and John Zamberlin. No matter how much success I might've had during a football game, there was always room to get better and that is a life lesson I will never forget.

To all of my teammates and leaders at Kforce (formerly Hall Kinion) who taught me so much and provided opportunities that I still can't believe have happened in my life. To Kelly Hansen for introducing me to the staffing and professional services industry. To Lisa Crawford and Angela Aronica for taking a chance on a kid who just wanted an opportunity to prove what he could do in the business world. To Erin Brawley for trusting a fellow trumpet player with your career. The work we performed together set the tone for what great teams can look like. To my entire local and national account team who supported my business efforts, I will never be able to say thank you enough. To Mary Jo Ferris for being a great teammate and travel buddy. I will never forget some of those crazy hotel lobby bar stories. To Jeffrey Neal, thank you for challenging me and helping me achieve 155! To Kye Mitchell, Joe Liberatore and David Dunkel, thank you for all of your support as the memories of working together will last a lifetime.

To all of my amazing customers for allowing me to build a relationship with you. Thank you for your trust in me and my team and for allowing us to create so many great business memories together. There are so many to thank but I wanted to mention a few that I became close with - Chris Bartsch, Clare Megathlin, Franci Boothby, Mark Cundy, Gilbert

Wong, Nuri Yalcin, Kimberly Sutherland, Joan Carravano, Nadine Holm, Andrea Sutton, Joel Austad, Jeff Dixon, Sara Straley, Kevin Raftery, John Starkweather, Tricia McKinley, Laura Downing, Mary Garcia, Cathy Mitchell, David Langston, Jeff Dixon, Ed Lambert, Tish St. Germain and Marc Johnson.

CUSTOMER AND COLLEAGUE TESTIMONIALS
(cited from LinkedIn)

"I have had the honor of working with Casey over the last 12 years and I have to say that I have enjoyed almost every minute of it! Casey and I worked together to develop one of the largest clients that our Firm has had. It was a lot of hard work to ensure that the client was always supported in ways that stretched the norm for Kforce. Casey pushes the envelope to make sure that services provided to the client are unique, help solve their biggest problems and ensures excellent delivery. His ability to work with clients by being authentic and genuinely caring about them sets him far apart from his competitors. People seek out Casey for his advice, his mentorship and for his uncanny wit. I can honestly say that I am a better leader for working with Casey and that he has provided some of the best times of my Sales career both professionally and personally."

-Mary Jo Ferris

"I worked with Casey and his team for several years while in an HR Manager position with a healthcare/IT firm. He provides quality service and has a great understanding of not only the overall technology industry needs, but needs that are specific to your organization."

-Cathy Mitchell

"Working with Casey has been a privilege during the Kforce Sales Strategy Transformation. As a senior executive and "champion" for this critical culture change initiative he has displayed humility, subject matter expertise, deep insight, strong critical thinking skills, emotional intelligence and finely-tuned listening skills in working closely with our consulting team at GrowthPlay. He personifies the very best of Kforce Values and is a catalyst for change, fun and new thinking focused on results. Looking forward to supporting him in his career journey which will be long and productive."

-Bill Taylor

"Casey exemplifies grace-under-fire in the difficult to navigate Fortune 100 space, and is one of the most service-oriented people I've ever encountered."

-Andrea Boff Sutton

"If you've worked with Casey, you know he's like no other. I've had the pleasure of working with Casey in one capacity or another since he started in the staffing industry. Casey raised the bar and set a high standard for other sales executives that reshaped the organization. Casey has a unique ability to build lasting relationships through his care for the partnership over his care for a deal. Casey's ability to mentor others resulted in growth of new account executives into top performers within the company.

One of his best traits though, his is sense of humor and the gift to keep light a conversation when we all take ourselves too seriously! Casey is a valued partner who will raise the bar in any endeavor he engages in."

-Jennifer Waldrip

"Working closely with Casey has given me the confidence to compete, share the story, and compete again. He has influenced me to not only work hard, but also share success or struggles, then turn the *page and go do it again. He's a true partner and a constant mentor."*

   -Kelly Hansen

SOCIAL MEDIA

Check out Casey's website to learn more about him, his podcast and how to hire him for speaking opportunities.

www.caseyjacox.com

The QB DadCast Podcast:
http://www.buzzsprout.com/766853

Twitter - @caseyjacox

LinkedIn – www.linkedin.com/caseyjacox

Instagram - @caseyjacox9 and @theqbdadcast

RESOURCES – ADDITIONAL REFERENCES FROM KEY BOOKS AND ARTICLES MENTIONED

- *"The Seven Habits of Highly Effective People"* by Stephen Covey, published August 15th, 1989

- *"Outliers: The Story of Success"* by Malcolm Gladwell, published, November 18th, 2008

- *"Premium Collection: Wisdom and Empowerment Series"* by Orison Swett Marden, published December 1st, 1894

- *"Ego Is The Enemy"* by Ryan Holiday, published June 14th, 2006

- "Be yourself, everyone else is already taken" by Mike Robbins, published March 23rd, 2009

- *"The Gifts of Imperfection"* by Brené Brown, published August 27th, 2010

- *"Who Moved My Cheese?* An Amazing Way to Deal with Change in Your Work and in Your Life" by Spencer Johnson, published

September 8th, 1998

- *"Grit"* by Angela Duckworth, published May 3rd, 2016

- *"Uncommon: Finding Your Path to Significance"* by Tony Dungy, published 2009

- *"Enchantment: The Art of Changing Hearts, Minds, and Action"* by Guy Kawasaki, published 2011

END NOTES

[1] Empathy," Lincoln College, accessed October 10, 2019, https://alccd.lincolncollege.edu/abraham-lincoln-character-qualities/empathy/.

[2] Brian Tracy, "The Golden Rule: How to Sell Like a Brilliant Sales Professional," Brian Tracy International, accessed September 17, 2019, https://www.briantracy.com/blog/sales-success/golden-rule-sales-performance-sales-professional/.

[3] Aja Frost, "75 Key Sales Statistics That'll Help You Sell Smarter in 2019," Hubspot, June 3, 2019, https://blog.hubspot.com/sales/sales-statistics.

[4] Julia Manoukian, "Only 18% of Buyers Trust and Respect Salespeople," SalesforLife, September 15, 2017, https://www.salesforlife.com/blog/only-18-percent-of-buyers-trust-and-respect-salespeople-roundup.

[5] 15 Inspiring Quotes from Sales Legends and Leaders," *High Velocity Sales*, February 7, 2015, https://highvelocitysales.wordpress.com/2015/02/07/15-inspiring-quotes-from-sales-legends/.

[6] John Kaplan, "Overcoming Seller Deficit Disorder," Force Management, August 26, 2009, http://customerthink.com/overcoming_seller_deficit_disorder/.

[7] "Active Listening Is a Sales Tool ... and Technology Can Help!" SalesLoft, accessed September 20, 2019,

https://salesloft.com/resources/blog/active-listening-sales-tool/.

[8] As quoted in Tom Gerencer, "200+ Sales Statistics You Must Know [Real Data for 2019 and Beyond]," Zety, December 25, 2018, https://zety.com/blog/sales-statistics.

[9] "'There's No I in Closer': How Top Performing Sales Reps Use Language to Close More Deals," Chorus, accessed September 20, 2019, https://resources.chorus.ai/blog/there-s-no-i-in-closer-how-top-performing-sales-reps-use-language-to-close-more-deals.

[10] "Vacation Car Dealer," YouTube video, posted February 25, 2015, 2:52, https://www.youtube.com/watch?v=HD6NCnwNQk4.

[11] Robert Clay, "Why You Must Follow Up Leads,," *Marketing Donut*, accessed September 23, 2019, https://www.marketingdonut.co.uk/sales/sales-techniques-and-negotiations/why-you-must-follow-up-leads.

[12] As quoted in Tom Gerencer, "200+ Sales Statistics You Must Know," https://zety.com/blog/sales-statistics#most-popular.

[13] CSO Insights, *Running Up the Down Escalator: 2017 CSO Insights World-Class Sales Practices Report* (Miller Heiman Group, 2017), 15.

[14] Emily Bauer, "20 Mind-Boggling Sales Statistics Every Sales Rep Needs to Know 2018," Propeller, April 19,

2017, https://www.propellercrm.com/blog/sales-statistics.

[15] "Why 8% of Sales People Get 80% of Sales," TickleTrain, accessed September 23, 2019, https://tickletrain.com/why-8-of-sales-people-get-80-of-sales/.

[16] Sam Holzman, "Social Selling Blog: Top 10 Social Selling Tools," *ZoomInfo Blog*, March 20, 2018, https://blog.zoominfo.com/top-10-social-selling-tools/.

[17] Todd Kunsman, "25 Social Selling Statistics that Matter for Sales Teams and Beyond," Propeller, October 30, 2018, https://everyonesocial.com/blog/social-selling-statistics/.

[18] Molly Clarke, "48 Shocking B2B Social Selling Statistics," *ZoomInfo Blog*, February 15, 2019, https://blog.zoominfo.com/20-shocking-social-selling-statistics/.

[19] Krysta Williams, "53 Sales Follow Up Statistics," *ZoomInfo Blog*, December 6, 2017, https://blog.zoominfo.com/sales-follow-up-statistics/.

[20] Brené Brown, "The Power of Vulnerability," video, 20:04, TED, accessed September 25, 2019, https://www.ted.com/talks/brene_brown_on_vulnerability.

[21] Thomas Metcalf, "Socratic Leadership Styles," *Chron*, accessed September 25, 2019, https://smallbusiness.chron.com/socratic-leadership-styles-69297.html.

[22] June D. Bell, "Firing for Online Behavior," Society of Human Resource Management, August 24, 2018, https://www.shrm.org/hr-today/news/hr-magazine/0918/pages/firing-for-online-behavior-.aspx.

[23] "More Than Half of Employers Have Found Content on Social Media That Caused Them NOT to Hire a Candidate, According to Recent CareerBuilder Survey" (press release), CareerBuilder, August 9, 2018, http://press.careerbuilder.com/2018-08-09-More-Than-Half-of-Employers-Have-Found-Content-on-Social-Media-That-Caused-Them-NOT-to-Hire-a-Candidate-According-to-Recent-CareerBuilder-Survey.

[24] "More Than Half of Employers Have Found Content on Social Media That Caused Them NOT to Hire a Candidate, According to Recent CareerBuilder Survey" (press release), CareerBuilder, August 9, 2018, http://press.careerbuilder.com/2018-08-09-More-Than-Half-of-Employers-Have-Found-Content-on-Social-Media-That-Caused-Them-NOT-to-Hire-a-Candidate-According-to-Recent-CareerBuilder-Survey.

[25] As quoted in Susan Steinbrecher, "35 Masterful Quotes to Inspire Healthier Workplace Relationships," *Entrepreneur,* March 14, 2016, https://www.entrepreneur.com/article/269762.

[26] Steinbrecher, "35 Masterful Quotes."

[27] Susan Halliwell, "42 Quotes to Inspire Persistence When Selling," *The Peak Blog,* December 1, 2014, https://www.peaksalesrecruiting.com/42-quotes-to-inspire-sales-persistence/.

[28] Angela Duckworth, "Grit: The Power of Passion and Perseverance," video, 6:01, TED, April 2013, https://www.ted.com/talks/angela_lee_duckworth_grit_the_power_of_passion_and_perseverance?language=en.

[29] "5 Characteristics of Grit: How Much Do You Have?" South African College of Applied Psychology, January 25, 2016, https://www.sacap.edu.za/blog/counselling/5-characteristics-of-grit-how-much-do-you-have/.

[30] "The Role of Resilience in the Workplace," Heads Up, August, 17, 2018, https://www.headsup.org.au/training-and-resources/news/2018/08/17/the-role-of-resilience-in-the-workplace.